What's Your Sign for PIZZA?

What's Your Sign for PIZZA?

*An Introduction to
Variation in
American Sign Language*

Ceil Lucas, Robert Bayley,
and Clayton Valli

Gallaudet University Press
Washington, D.C.

Gallaudet University Press

Washington, DC 20002

http://gupress.gallaudet.edu

© 2003 by Gallaudet University

Printed in the United States of America

15 14 13 12 11 10 09 08   2 3 4 5 6 7 8 9 10

Cover photographs of Brenda Keller, Zavier Sabió, and Hatim A. Vali
by Jonathan Kerr.

Library of Congress Cataloging-in-Publication Data

Lucas, Ceil.

   What's your sign for pizza? : an introduction to variation in American Sign
   Language / Ceil Lucas, Robert Bayley, and Clayton Valli.

      p.   cm.

   Includes bibliographic references and index.

   ISBN –13: 978-1-56368–144-8   ISBN-10: 1-56368-144-7

      1. American Sign Language.   I.   Bayley, Robert, 1943–   II. Valli, Clayton.

   III. Title.

HV2474.L835   2003

419'.7 — dc21

                                                            2003049210

∞ The paper used in this publication meets the minimum requirements of
American National Standard for Information Sciences — Permanence of Paper for
Printed Library Materials, ANSI Z39.48–1984.

This project is dedicated to Clayton Valli, in loving memory.

Contents

Preface ix

Introduction 1

1. Some Basic Concepts about Language 3
2. Signs Have Parts 12
3. Variation: Basic Concepts 17
4. Phonological Variation 23
5. Syntactic Variation 41
6. Lexical Variation 46
7. Collecting Variable Data 54
8. Summary and Conclusions 57

Notes 59

Supplementary Readings 61

The Importance of Variation Research for Deaf Communities 63
Ceil Lucas and Robert Bayley

Lexical Variation in African American and White Signing 83
Ceil Lucas, Robert Bayley, Ruth Reed, and Alyssa Wulf

Sociolinguistic Variation 111
Ceil Lucas, Robert Bayley, Clayton Valli, Mary Rose, and Alyssa Wulf

Index 181

Preface

Welcome to *What's Your Sign for PIZZA? An Introduction to Variation in American Sign Language.* These materials are designed to introduce members of the Deaf community and the general public to sociolinguistic variation in American Sign Language (ASL). We have published a technical report about the project, but researchers in linguistics also have a clear responsibility to give back to the communities that have so generously shared their language, whether spoken or signed. These materials represent our modest gift to the Deaf community.

The materials are part of a large project that started in 1994. The production of these materials is supported by the National Science Foundation, with a supplement to Research Awards SBR #9310116 and SBR #9709522. We are grateful to the National Science Foundation for this support. In addition, Robert Bayley's participation was partially supported by a UTSA Faculty Development Leave Award. We would also like to thank Jim Dellon, Ron Reed, and Rosemary Bennett of the Gallaudet University Television and Media Production Services for the production of the videotape and Robert Hahn and Raymond Raney for the voiceover. We thank Dr. Barbara Bodner-Johnson for her valuable feedback on the materials and the organizers of Deaf Way II for giving us the opportunity to do the Special Interest Group at which we pilot-tested the materials. We are grateful to Ivey Wallace, Deirdre Mullervy, and Carol Hoke of Gallaudet University Press for their role in the production of the materials. Finally, we heartily thank all of the people who participated in the project—without their generous participation the project simply would not have been possible. Everyone who appears in the clips has given written permission for the clips to be used.

Introduction

In recent years both Deaf and hearing people have become more aware of the diversity of the Deaf community in the United States, which now includes people in virtually all occupations and of many national origins. In this book, designed to be used with the accompanying compact disc (CD), we celebrate another dimension of diversity in the U.S. Deaf community: variation in language, specifically, variation in the way Deaf people all across the United States use ASL.

Variation in language means that people have different ways of saying or signing the same thing. In spoken English, for example, some people say "soda," whereas others say "pop," "Coke," or "soft drink"; some people say "sofa" while others say "couch" or "davenport." In ASL there are many signs for BIRTHDAY, HALLOWEEN, and EARLY. In this book we explore the different kinds of variation in ASL. Before we focus on variation we explain some fundamental concepts about all human language and discuss the basic structure of signs because these determine the ways that language can vary.

This book is based on a large research project that lasted from 1994 to 2001.[1] Deaf ASL users from seven different areas in the United States, ranging in age from thirteen to ninety-three, were videotaped while they chatted. Many of them were also interviewed. The seven areas are Boston, Massachusetts; Frederick, Maryland; Staunton, Virginia; New Orleans, Louisiana; Kansas City, Missouri, and Olathe, Kansas; Fremont and San Jose, California; and Bellingham, Washington. In all, 207 people took part in the project. Participants included men and women and African Americans and Caucasians from both Deaf and hearing families. The examples of signing that you will see on the video come from the project tapes. That is, the examples come from videotaped interactions among signers in different parts of the United States that were recorded under a wide variety of conditions. The ideas about variation in ASL in this book are based on what we found during our analysis of the tapes.

How to Use These Materials

These materials consist of a CD and this accompanying guide, and they are designed to be used together. Both the CD and the guide provide an introduction to basic concepts about languages and variation and specific examples of variation in ASL. We advise reading a section of the guide and then watching the corresponding section of the CD. Another approach would be to first watch the CD all the way through, then read each section of the guide, and then go back and watch the corresponding section of the CD again. We have provided links in the guide to the clips that you will see. For example, when examples of the sign DEAF are shown on the CD, you will find a note in the guide and an explanation of exactly what you have seen on the CD. You will also notice that some of the sections of the CD are separated by clips of individuals signing. These clips are not specifically discussed in the guide, but they further illustrate the richness of variation in ASL. At the end of each major section we have provided questions for discussion. The final section of the guide consists of three supplemental readings that provide further information on variation in both spoken and signed languages and in the text itself. Within these readings you will occasionally see footnote numbers. These numbers refer to specific references listed at the end of the text. We've designed these materials to be used both in a classroom setting and on an individual basis.

1

Some Basic Concepts about Language

Before we present differences in the ways that Deaf people in various regions of the United States sign and how the same person may use different forms of a sign on different occasions, we need to describe some of the distinctive features of all human languages, including of course ASL and other signed languages, and to distinguish between human languages and other types of communication systems. We also briefly sketch the history of ASL to show the relationships between the language varieties found throughout the United States. As we shall see, one of the distinguishing features of all human languages is that languages, in contrast to other communication systems with which they share some characteristics, are always changing. And we shall also see that one of the main distinguishing features of human languages is that they vary. That is, people have different ways of signing or saying the same thing.

⊙

Clip 1. The concepts discussed here are also covered in the Basic Concepts section of the CD.

⊙

LANGUAGE IS A COMMUNICATION SYSTEM

Language is a rule-governed communication system.[2] A communication system is a system that people use to share information. When a system is based on rules that its users know and follow, it is called a **rule-governed**

system. Examples of other communication systems include Morse code, which uses either sound or light, semaphore (the flag system the U.S. Navy uses), traffic signals, and signs on highways and in public places. Many animals such as birds, bees, and dolphins also have communication systems.

Language has much in common with all of these systems. For example, all of these systems are composed of symbols. The combinations of dots and dashes in Morse code, for example, are symbols for English letters. The signs that we see on highways and in public places are also symbols. Spoken English words are symbols made up of a combination of sounds, and English letters are written symbols for sounds. And ASL signs are symbols (see Figure 1).

These symbols are organized and used systematically. For example, in ASL, when a sign is made with two hands and the two handshapes are different, only one hand, referred to as the *dominant* hand, can move. We see this in the signs MONEY and WORD. (Note the convention of writing the English words for signs in small capital letters.) In MONEY, the hand that moves is shaped like a Flat O, and the nondominant hand is shaped like

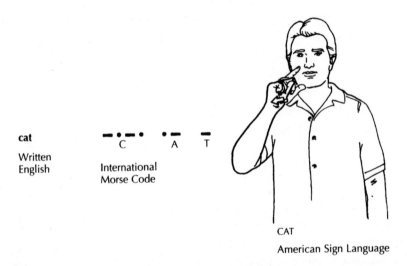

cat
Written
English

C   A   T
International
Morse Code

CAT
American Sign Language

Figure 1. Symbolic representation of "cat." Note: This is one of several variants of the sign CAT.

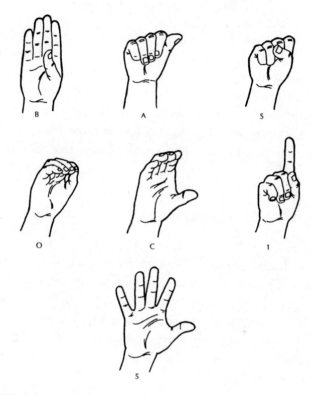

Figure 2. The seven basic handshapes of the passive hand

an Open B. Only the Flat O handshape moves. In WORD, the dominant hand is shaped like a G, while the nondominant hand is shaped like a 1. Only the G moves. The nondominant hand in two-handed signs tends to be one of seven handshapes: B, A, S, O, C, 1, and 5 (see Figure 2).

The forms of the symbols that make up a communication system may be arbitrary or iconic. *Arbitrary* means that the actual form of the symbol does not reflect the form of the thing or activity that it symbolizes. The form of the ASL sign WRONG is arbitrary, and the spoken form of the English word *door* is also arbitrary. *Iconic* means that the form of the symbol is an icon or picture of some aspect of the thing or activity it symbolizes. The forms of the ASL signs TREE, TABLE, and many others are iconic. In spoken English, words such as *choo-choo, meow,* and *cock-a-doodle-doo* are iconic.

The symbols of a communication system are shared by members of a community. Users of ASL form a community, and they share a system that is different from the one shared by users of British Sign Language (BSL) or Australian Sign Language (AUSLAN). There may also be smaller communities within the larger community, thus signers from California may use signs that signers from Connecticut do not know or use; moreover, as we will see, African American signers may use signs that white signers do not use.

LANGUAGE HAS SOME UNIQUE CHARACTERISTICS

Language has some characteristics that make it unique. For example, language is **productive**, whereas other communication systems are limited in the number of messages they can produce. The number of sentences and messages that can be produced with the symbols of human language is infinite. It is impossible to even try to count how many sentences can be produced in a given language. Every day you see sentences that you have never seen before, and you produce sentences that have never been produced before.

Language is composed of symbols and has ways of showing the **relationship between symbols.** For example, English has a class of words called *prepositions* that shows the relationship between other words. In the sentence "The book is on the table," the word "on" shows the relationship between the words "book" and "table." This relationship is shown in ASL with *classifier predicates,* so a signer might sign BOOK and TABLE and then use a handshape and a movement that represents the placing of the book on the table.

Although the set of symbols that other communication systems use is limited and set, language permits the continual **introduction of new symbols.** New symbols are often introduced into ASL by means of fingerspelling. Recent examples of this are #FAX and #EMAIL (of course, the English words themselves are also fairly new). Two signs that already exist can also be combined to create a new sign in a process known as *compounding.* Older examples of compounds in ASL are EAT⁀SLEEP ("home")

American Sign Language: ITALY   Italian Sign Language: ITALY

Figure 3. The ASL and Italian Sign Language signs for ITALY

and BOY⌢SAME ("brother"); a fairly recent addition is DEAF⌢WAY.* New signs are also added to the language as a result of ontact with other languages. Many American signs for countries are now being abandoned in favor of the country's own sign, as we see with the sign for ITALY (see Figure 3).

Users of other communication systems generally use their systems to communicate about essential survival or emergency management, but language can be used for an **unrestricted number of domains.** That is, language can be used to talk about any topic, from survival and emergencies to philosophy, physics, and art. The symbols that make up a language can be broken down into smaller parts, and sometimes these smaller parts have independent meanings. For example, one part of each sign is its handshape. The signs LOUSY and AWKWARD have a 3 handshape, while the sign PREACH has a 9 or F handshape. In these signs the handshape itself has no specific meaning. But in the signs for THREE-MONTHS, THREE-DOLLARS, and NINE-WEEKS, these same handshapes have the specific meaning of a number.

* The # symbol is used to show the difference between a fingerspelled loan sign and a regular sign. A loan sign is a combination of signs for English letters and ASL movements. The ⌢ symbol indicates that the two signs make up a compound sign.

7

In other communication systems, each symbol or group of symbols usually has one meaning. In language, **a symbol or a group of symbols may convey more than one meaning**. For example, the sequence of signs HOME YOU may have different meanings depending on the facial expression of the signer and the situation in which the signs are produced. It may be a yes/no question ("Are you home?") or a statement ("You're home.") or even a command ("Go home!"). Users of a language can refer to the past, future, and nonimmediate, unlike other communication systems, which are generally restricted to the present or immediate.

Language **naturally changes across time**, unlike other communication systems. We see, for example, that some two-handed signs such as COW have become one handed; the active hand of the sign HELP used to be placed on the elbow but now has moved up to the base hand; the base handshape in one form of TOMATO has changed from a Flat O to a 1 handshape. These changes, moreover, do not happen all at once. Rather, for a long time, two (or more) signs may be used in a community, with younger members using more of the new signs than older members. In many cases the change from one sign to another (or from one form of a sign to another) takes many years. This type of change is characteristic of every living language.

Just as language varies over time, it also varies across geographical and social space. People in Boston, for example, may sign differently from the way that people in New Orleans do, and people in California may use signs (or forms of signs) that are different from those that people in Washington, D.C., use. Regional differences are not the only influences that show themselves in different ways of signing (or of speaking). **Social influences** also play major roles in signers' choices between different signs or versions of the same sign. For example, in most languages that linguists have studied carefully, women and men sign or speak differently. Older people use signs that are different from the ones younger people use, and members of different ethnic groups sometimes prefer different signs or forms of signs.

Another difference between a language and other communication systems occurs in the **range of styles**, or **registers**, that characterize all human languages. In written English, for example, when we are writing a letter to apply for a job we choose words and use conventions that are different from the ones we use when we're writing a letter or an email to a close friend. And, in ASL and other sign languages, when we are at home relaxing with friends and family we express ourselves differently from the way we do when we are meeting with our supervisor at work.

In contrast to other communication systems, language can be **used interchangeably.** All users of a language can send and receive messages. This is not true, though, of animal communication systems. For example, only male birds sing, and only foraging bees, the ones who hunt for food, dance.

Language users also **monitor their use**—that is, they listen to or watch themselves as they produce language and correct themselves if they feel they have made a mistake. For example, when signers feel that they have produced an incorrect sign, they may sign I MEAN or BACK-UP and then sign what they meant.

One very important feature of language is that **parts of the system must be learned by interacting with other users.** Even though a good deal of research has shown that humans are born with an innate capacity to learn and use language, children must interact with adults and with other children to learn their language completely. This is of course extremely important for deaf children. Since they do not have access to spoken language, deaf children need to be exposed to a visual language such as ASL as early as possible. Users of language can also learn other variants of the same language. For example, a signer from one part of the United States can move to another part and learn the signs used exclusively in that area. Signers can also learn other sign languages—an ASL user can learn Italian Sign Language or Thai Sign Language.

Finally, language users **think about and discuss language.** They write dictionaries, grammar books, and linguistics textbooks, and they make videotapes and write books about variation in sign language. This feature seems to be unique to the human species. Thus we see from our discussion of the differences between a language and other communication systems that ASL is a natural language that members of the North American Deaf community use. It is a language that has developed over time among a community of users. It exhibits all of the features that make languages unique communication systems.

A HISTORICAL SKETCH OF ASL

Not much is known about the deaf people who lived in North America before the nineteenth century, but some probably came from Great Britain and Europe, and some were probably born here. Deaf people who came from other countries probably brought their sign languages with them, and other communities of deaf people living in America probably developed their own sign languages. In 1817 Thomas Hopkins Gallaudet and Laurent Clerc established the Connecticut Asylum for the Education and Instruction of Deaf and Dumb Persons—now called the American School for the Deaf—in Hartford, Connecticut.[3] Gallaudet met Clerc when he traveled to Europe in search of a method for educating Alice Cogswell, the deaf daughter of his neighbor, Dr. Mason Cogswell. He went first to Great Britain to learn about the oral method used by the Braidwood Schools in Scotland and near London, but the school directors' conditions for learning the method were so restrictive that Gallaudet decided not to stay.

While in London, Gallaudet met a Frenchman by the name of Sicard, who was the director of the Royal Institution for the Deaf in Paris. Sicard was in London with two of his deaf students, Jean Massieu and Laurent Clerc, demonstrating the success of his teaching methods. The method used at the Royal Institution involved the use of French Sign Language along with a set of signs invented to represent parts of written and spoken French not found in French Sign Language. These so-called methodical signs had originally been developed by Abbé de l'Epée, the founder and first director of the school in Paris. Sicard invited Gallaudet to the Royal Institution to learn French Sign Language and the teaching method he and his colleagues used in France. Gallaudet accepted Sicard's offer and spent several months in Paris. When he returned to America, he was accompanied by Laurent Clerc. On the trip to America, Clerc continued teaching Gallaudet French Sign Language and Gallaudet taught Clerc English.

Many deaf people and some hearing people came to Hartford to learn the teaching method in use at the newly established school. Some of the deaf students who came to Hartford, such as the ones from Martha's

Vineyard, brought their own sign language with them. They also learned the sign language the school was using, which no doubt included many French signs. This combination of community sign languages and French Sign Language became the basis for American Sign Language. As students graduated, many became teachers in other schools for the deaf, thus spreading ASL across the country. For example, in 1821 Abigail Dillingham, one of the first graduates of the Hartford school, moved to Philadelphia to become a teacher at the new Pennsylvania Institution. The career of Hartford graduate William Willard provides a very good example of how graduates of the American School for the Deaf (ASD) spread ASL throughout the country. Willard was a student at the Hartford school from 1824 to 1829. After graduation he became a teacher at the Ohio School for the Deaf until 1841 and later moved to Indiana, where he became the first principal of the school for the deaf in that state.

ASL is very different from systems such as Signing Exact English (SEE) that were developed to represent English on the hands for use in deaf education. (These systems are also commonly known as Manually Coded English, or MCE.) ASL and other sign languages are also distinct from the gestures found in many spoken languages. Research on the structure and use of ASL began in the 1960s, with the work of William C. Stokoe.

DISCUSSION QUESTIONS

1. Language permits the introduction of new symbols. List as many new ASL signs as you can and explain where they come from.

2. Language changes naturally over time. List two signs that have changed and describe how they have done so.

3. Observe someone self-correcting while signing. How does the person indicate that she is correcting herself?

4. Do you know other sign languages? How did you learn them?

2

Signs Have Parts

The symbols that make up languages can be broken down into smaller parts. The signs of sign languages have several parts. ASL signs have five basic parts: handshape, movement, location, palm orientation, and non-manual signals (facial expressions). Different signs may have the same part. For example, the sign FEEL has the same handshape as the sign SICK, the same movement as the sign HAPPY, and the same location as the sign COMPLAIN. We know that these parts are important because a change in one part may create a difference in meaning. For example, the signs SUMMER, DRY, and UGLY share the same handshape, movement, and palm orientation, but they differ in location. We know which sign is being signed by the location. Similarly, RED and CUTE share the same location, movement, and palm orientation but differ in handshape; SHORT and TRAIN share everything except for palm orientation, while SIT and CHAIR differ only in movement. When pieces of a language are responsible for a difference in meaning in this way, they are said to be *contrastive*. (See Figure 4.)

⊙

Clip 2. The concepts discussed here are also covered in the Signs Have Parts section of the CD.

⊙

Nonmanual signals may also be contrastive. The signs LATE and NOT YET are often distinguished only by the facial expression that accompanies them. Many signs are not correctly produced without a nonmanual signal. For example, the sign meaning "finally" and often glossed as PAH requires

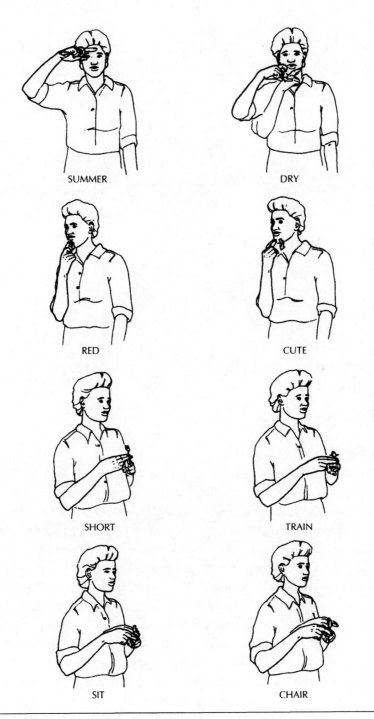

Figure 4. Pairs of signs that differ in only one parameter

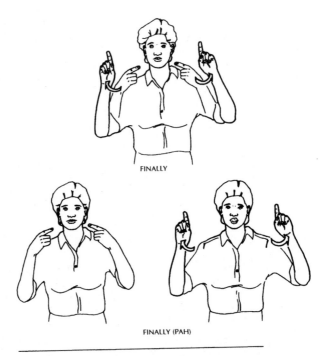

FINALLY

FINALLY (PAH)

Figure 5. Two versions of FINALLY

the mouth to open during the production of the sign; NOT YET is usually made with the mouth open and the tongue slightly out (see Figure 5).

Just as words in spoken languages are made up of sequences of vowels and consonants, the signs in sign languages are made up of sequences of movements and holds.[4] *Holds* are periods of time during which all aspects of the sign are in a steady state, not changing, while *movements* are periods of time during which some part of the sign is changing. More than one part can change at once. For example, in UNDERSTAND, only the handshape changes; in MISS, both the location and the handshape change. The sign DEAF is composed of a hold, then a movement, and then a hold. The sign can begin at the ear and move down to the chin, but it can also start at the chin and move up to the ear. Holds and movements are called *segments*, and each segment has parts: handshape, location, palm orientation, and non-manual signal information. Figure 6 shows an abstract representation of the parts of the sign DEAF in the form that is used in ASL dictionaries.

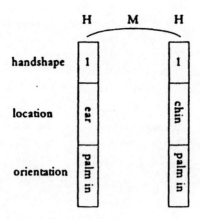

Figure 6. The structure of the sign DEAF

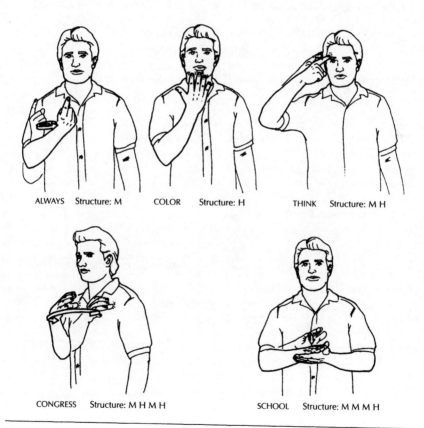

ALWAYS   Structure: M   COLOR   Structure: H   THINK   Structure: M H

CONGRESS   Structure: M H M H   SCHOOL   Structure: M M M H

Figure 7. Examples of possible sign structure

The structure of DEAF is hold-movement-hold (H M H). DEAF has a 1 handshape, and the palm is generally oriented inward. In standard or dictionary form, the sign begins just below the ear and ends near the corner of the mouth. It thus has two locations. In standard form, the first location is at the ear and the second in the area of the chin. Of course, the hold-movement-hold structure of DEAF is only one of many possible combinations of movement and hold segments. Figure 7 illustrates some other possibilities.

This way of analyzing signs as sequences of movements and holds, each of which can be further described depending on the handshape, location, palm orientation, and nonmanual signals, proves to be very useful for describing variation in ASL, as we shall see in the next section.

DISCUSSION QUESTIONS

1. For each of the following signs, find another sign that has the same features for handshape, movement, and location:

	Same Handshape	Same Movement	Same Location
Example: FEEL	SICK	HAPPY	MY
FORGET			
CUTE			
ENJOY			
WORSE			
DISCUSS			

2. What feature differs between the signs in each of the following pairs?
   a. SUMMER/DRY   c. SHORT/TRAIN
   b. RED/CUTE   d. SIT/CHAIR

3

Variation: Basic Concepts

Variation refers to alternative ways of signing or saying the same thing. As we mentioned at the beginning of this book, "sofa," "couch," and "davenport" are three different ways of referring to the same piece of furniture in spoken English, while "soda," "pop," and "soft drink" are various ways of referring to the same beverage. As we also mentioned, there are many different signs for HALLOWEEN and BIRTHDAY. Linguistic *variables* are alternatives for signing or saying the same thing. These alternatives may correlate with the social characteristics of the signer or speaker, in which case we talk about *sociolinguistic* variables. For example, signers from ASL-signing families often prefer the form of the verb KNOW that is produced on the forehead, whereas signers from nonsigning families often prefer the form that is produced below the forehead or even near the mouth.

⊙

Clip 3. The concepts discussed here are also covered in the Variation: Basic Concepts section of the CD.

⊙

We see variation in all parts of the language. In what we call **phonological variation,** the variation that affects the basic parts of signs, units can be changed, added, removed, or rearranged. In terms of change, the individual parts of signs can be variable: The **handshape** of FUNNY and BORED may or may not have the thumb extended, while YESTERDAY and WONDER may be signed with the pinky extended. **Location** may also vary, so KNOW, for example, may be signed on the forehead or further down on the cheek; WEEK may be signed with the **palm orientation** down or up. Some forms of a sign such as HELP may have internal **movement** that other forms of the sign do not. And since signers have two hands available to them, we can expect variation in the **number of hands** used in a sign. Some two-handed signs such as DEER may be signed with only one hand while others such as RIGHT may substitute a table or the signer's knee for the second hand. Other signs such as DIE were originally signed with one hand and have become two handed.

You will recall that signs are composed of sequences of movements and holds. Each movement or hold is known as a segment, and **segments can be added or left out** in the course of signing. For example, GOOD consists of a hold, a movement, and a hold; IDEA consists of a movement and a hold. In the phrase GOOD IDEA, the last hold of GOOD is deleted, that is, it disappears. Likewise, one form of FATHER is a hold with internal movement—the fingers wiggle; one form of STUDY is also a hold with internal movement. But in the phrase FATHER STUDY, a movement is added between the two holds. This addition is called movement **epenthesis.**[5]

Sometimes a combination of a movement and a hold may be deleted in what resembles the **syllable deletion** that occurs in spoken languages. An older form of SNOW, for example, consists of WHITE followed by wiggling fingers, representing falling snow. It is common now to see only the second part of the sign. Likewise, an older form of DOG consists of the hand slapping the upper thigh, followed by the middle finger rubbing the thumb, palm up. Again, this second part of the sign frequently occurs by itself.

The parts of signs can also be **rearranged.** For example, DEAF consists of a hold at the ear, a movement downward, and then a hold on the lower cheek. However, it is common for the first hold to be at the lower cheek and for the sign to move up and end at the ear. This rearrangement of the location is called **metathesis** and is similar to what users of spoken languages do when they say "hunderd" instead of "hundred." It is interesting to note that not all signs allow the kind of rearrangement that can occur in DEAF, where the positions of the two holds are reversed. Rather, this kind of rearrangement seems to be acceptable for signs made on a horizontal plane, such as FLOWER, RESTAURANT, and HONEYMOON, but other signs like DEAF, such as INDIAN and YESTERDAY, allow movement only up but not down. Interestingly, these signs are produced on a vertical plane.

In addition to variation in parts of segments, segments, and combinations of segments, we also see variation in word-sized units, that is, where the variation affects the whole sign. This is what we see in **lexical variation.** We mentioned the many different signs for HALLOWEEN and BIRTHDAY, and in most cases we are talking about signs that are completely different from each other. For example, the sign for BIRTHDAY in which the ear is tugged does not share anything except meaning with the sign for BIRTHDAY that is a compound of the signs BIRTH and DAY; the sign for HALLOWEEN that has two V handshapes over the eyes is completely different from the one in which the middle finger of the active hand thumps the back of the base hand. Later on we will compare this to several signs for BANANA that share the same location, palm orientation, and base hand and differ only in the handshape of the active hand.

Variation in word-sized units also occurs at the level of sentences. ASL is known as a "pro-drop" language (like Chinese, Italian, and Spanish); that is, the verb in a sentence may be accompanied by a pronoun, but the pronoun may also be left out. Here is an example: The sentence PRO.1 THINK, meaning "I think," can also be signed simply THINK, with no pronoun.* This is an example of **syntactic variation.**

Most of the types of variation we have described so far may occur within the signing of individuals. To be sure, people may have a preferred sign for BIRTHDAY, for example, and always use that sign, just as some speakers of English may always refer to a particular piece of furniture as a "davenport," whereas others may always refer to it as a "couch" or a "sofa." Other people may use a variety of signs for a single concept such as BIRTHDAY,

---

* PRO.1 refers to the first-person pronoun "I." Similarly, PRO.2 refers to the second-person pronoun "you" and PRO.3 refers to the third-person pronouns "he," "she," "it," or "they."

depending on the situation and the person to whom they are talking. The signing of most people, however, varies at the phonological and syntactic levels. For example, even people who usually sign DEAF from the ear to the chin will occasionally use the chin-to-ear form. Most people who usually use the standard dictionary form of signs made with a 1 handshape will sometimes use an L handshape or a 5 handshape for a pronoun. Even people who seldom use the standard dictionary forms will sometimes use the ear-to-chin form of DEAF and the 1 handshape form of a personal pronoun such as "I." Thus, when we study variation in ASL or any other language, we are not looking at **categorical** differences in the language that different people or groups of people use. That is, we are not saying that some people always sign one way and others always sign another way. Rather, what we are interested in is discovering what kind of people (for example, middle-aged white women who live in Kansas) usually sign one way, whereas other people (for example, young African American men in California) usually choose a different version of the same sign.

Finally, as linguists, our orientation is **descriptive** rather than **prescriptive**. That is, our job is to describe the way that people actually sign rather than prescribe how people should sign. When we say that people in one region use the standard dictionary form of a sign more often than people in another region, we are not implying that the signing of people who use the standard form (for example, the ear-to-chin form of DEAF) more often is any better than the signing of people who use a different form (for example, the chin-to-ear form of DEAF). Rather, in the case of ASL, as with all languages, the decision as to what constitutes ASL, or "good" ASL, belongs to those to whom the language belongs—the diverse members of the North American Deaf community.

HOW DO WE EXPLAIN THE VARIATION?

We have described some examples of variation in ASL—for example, the sign DEAF, which can be signed from ear to chin or from chin to ear, the sign KNOW, which can be signed at the forehead or on the cheek, and the sign YESTERDAY, in which the pinky can be extended or not. Linguists try to figure out what accounts for or explains the variation. Is there something about the sign immediately before or immediately after it that contributes to the variation? Is there something about the signer—where he is from, his family background—that helps explain the variation? The characteristics of the context in which the sign is used and the social background of the signer that may help explain the variation are known as **constraints**. There are two kinds of constraints. **Linguistic constraints,** also known as internal constraints, are ones that have to do specifically with language structure. The sign—or parts of it—that occurs immediately before or immediately after the variable sign may be a constraint; the grammatical function of the variable itself may be a constraint—that is, whether the sign is a noun, a verb, or an adjective. The type of discourse in which the variable occurs—for example, a conversation, a story, or a lecture—may play a role, and whether the sign receives stronger emphasis than other signs may also influence a signer's choice of one form over another. **Social constraints,** also known as external constraints, are social characteristics such as region, gender, age, ethnicity, and socioeconomic class that correlate with the variation. For example, women may use a variant more often than men do, or older signers may use a variant less often than younger signers do. There may be differences between African American signing and Caucasian signing. Moreover, certain social factors such as a signer's language background are of particular importance in understanding variation in sign languages. That is, does a signer come from a signing, ASL background or from a hearing, nonsigning background? Whether a signer is Deaf-Blind or sighted may also be a factor.

Variation, then, is subject to many influences found in the linguistic environment (for example, the handshapes of the preceding and following signs), the occasion on which the sign is used (a conversation among close friends or a response to a question during a job interview), and the personal characteristics of the signer. Also, all of these influences are at work at the same time. That is, it is very difficult, for example, to disentangle the social characteristics of the signer. A young female African American signer from a Deaf family in New Orleans is *always* young and female and African American and from a Deaf family in New Orleans. All of these characteristics—or only some of them—might influence her choice of one form of a sign or another. For this reason linguists who study variation use complicated statistical software to sort out the extent to which the different characteristics of the signer influence that person's choice among different versions of the same sign and to evaluate the relative importance of those characteristics. In this way we are able to discover the degree to which the variation is systematic, that is, predictable from the context in which a sign is used and from the social characteristics of the signer. We are also able to make statements about the relative importance of the various influences on a signer's choices.

WHY IS VARIATION IMPORTANT?

All natural languages exhibit variation. By describing the patterned, rule-governed variation in sign languages, we can see that they are real languages. Although earlier generations of American Deaf people sometimes accepted and internalized the negative attitudes of the mainstream society about sign language, Deaf people now are proud to recognize ASL as a language like any other, and part of what makes ASL a real language is the presence of variation. The description of variation also helps us to see whether there are any **modality** differences, that is, whether the variation in sign languages differs in any way from that in spoken languages. Also, languages change naturally over time, and variation is usually the first step in the direction of change. By studying variation we can begin to understand how languages change.

4

Phonological Variation

We turn now to examples of variation from the project on which this book and the accompanying CD are based. These examples come from the videotapes we made during a project that began in 1994. We traveled to seven U.S. sites: Staunton, Virginia; Frederick, Maryland; Boston, Massachusetts; New Orleans, Louisiana; Kansas City, Missouri, and Olathe, Kansas; Fremont, California; and Bellingham, Washington (see Figure 8).

⊙

Clip 4. The project, as well as phonological variation, are also described on the CD.

⊙

We chose these sites because they all have thriving communities of ASL users. In addition, Staunton, Frederick, Boston, Fremont, and Olathe are the sites of residential schools for deaf children. We chose these seven areas in order to represent the major geographic areas of the United States—northeast, east, south, midwest, west, and northwest. We video-taped a total of 207 people in groups. Some groups had 2 people; others had as many as 7. For the first part of the videotaping, people just chatted without the researchers present. Most of the people knew each other, so they could talk about shared experiences and current events.

After they had chatted for about an hour, we selected two people from each group. Then we interviewed these people in depth about their

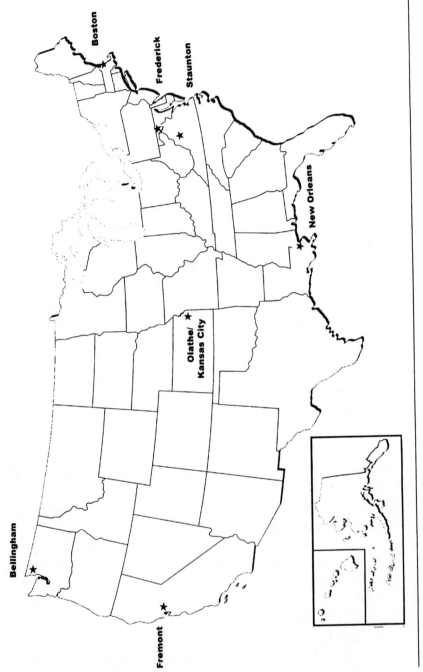

Figure 8. The research sites

language backgrounds, their educational and work experiences, and their family lives. We then showed them a set of pictures, asking them what their signs were for the objects or actions represented in the pictures. In four of the sites—Boston, New Orleans, Kansas City/Olathe, and Fremont—both African American and Caucasian signers participated in the study. In Staunton, Frederick, and Bellingham, where relatively few African American people live, we interviewed only Caucasian signers. We interviewed people in three age groups: 15–25, 26–54, and 55 and older. We chose these specific age groups because they parallel the developments in deaf education. People who were 55 and older were educated at a time when state schools for deaf students focused on oralism and prohibited the use of ASL in the classroom.

When people in the 26–54 group were going through school, ASL was beginning to gain recognition as a language, and many schools were beginning to follow the philosophy of Total Communication, that is, signing and talking at the same time. Many of the signers in the youngest group have been able to use ASL in the classroom.

We tried to get even numbers of men and women, and we videotaped both working-class and middle-class people. For our study "working class" means that the participants had gone to a residential school but had not continued their education after that, had settled in the area of the school, and were working in blue-collar jobs. The "middle-class" group consisted of people who had continued on to college after completing the residential school, had maybe left the area, but, if so, had been back in the area for at least ten years and were working in white-collar jobs. The youngest signers, who were still in school, were grouped with their parents in determining their social class. Of the 207 people in the study, 45 were from deaf families. Figure 9 shows the project at a glance.

We collected examples of three variables from the videotapes: the sign DEAF, which varies in its location; signs such as KNOW, which also vary in their location; and signs made with a 1 handshape, which vary in many ways. We selected examples of these signs because they occur on the tapes frequently (and in everyday signing), and we knew that we would have enough examples of them for statistical analysis. From our observations of

A seven-year project on sociolinguistic variation in ASL.
(June 1, 1994–July 31, 2001)

OVERVIEW OF DATA COLLECTION:

Sites Visited:

1. Staunton, Va.
2. Frederick, Md.
3. Boston, Mass.
4. New Orleans, La.
5. Fremont, Calif.
6. Olathe, Kans./Kansas City, Mo.
7. Bellingham, Wash.

Twelve groups at each site, except for Virginia, Maryland, and Washington (only Caucasian groups)

African American Groups:		Caucasian Groups:	
Middle Class	Working Class	Middle Class	Working Class
15–25	15–25	15–25	15–25
26–54	26–54	26–54	26–54
55+	55+	55+	55+

A total of 207 ASL signers (Each group consisted of 2–6 signers)

OVERALL GOAL OF THE PROJECT:

A description of phonological, morphosyntactic, and lexical variation in ASL and the correlation of variation with external factors such as age, region, gender, ethnicity, and socioeconomic status

Figure 9. The project at a glance

the videotapes we also knew that these signs varied a great deal, and we wanted to understand what was behind the variation.

DEAF

In ASL, the sign DEAF can be signed from the ear to the chin and also from the chin to the ear, as we mentioned earlier. In the course of our analysis, however, we discovered a third form of DEAF, in which the index finger does not move down or up but simply contacts the lower cheek. These are all illustrated in Figure 10. The form of DEAF that goes from ear to chin is called the **citation form.** This is the form that is usually found in sign language dictionaries and taught in sign language classes. The chin-to-ear and contact-cheek forms are known as **noncitation forms.** that is, they differ from the dictionary form in one or more respects.

⊙

> **Clip 5.** We see four examples of DEAF on the CD: (1) The woman on the right signs BOSTON DEAF CLUB (an older form of the sign for "club," which looks like SET-UP), with DEAF moving from ear to chin; (2) the man in the middle signs DEAF HELP, DEAF SUPPORT, with the contact-cheek form of DEAF; (3) the man signs FIND DEAF, PICK++, with the chin-to-ear form of the sign; and (4) the woman on the left signs KNOW PRO.1 ("me") DEAF, also with the chin-to-ear form.

⊙

We collected a total of 1,618 tokens, or examples, from our video-tapes. We looked at each token and noted four things:

1. The grammatical function of the sign DEAF: DEAF can be an adjective, as in the phrase DEAF CAT; it can also function as a noun, as in the sentence DEAF UNDERSTAND, which might be translated into English as "Deaf people understand." It can function as a predicate, as in the sentence PRO.1 DEAF, "I am Deaf," and it also appears in many

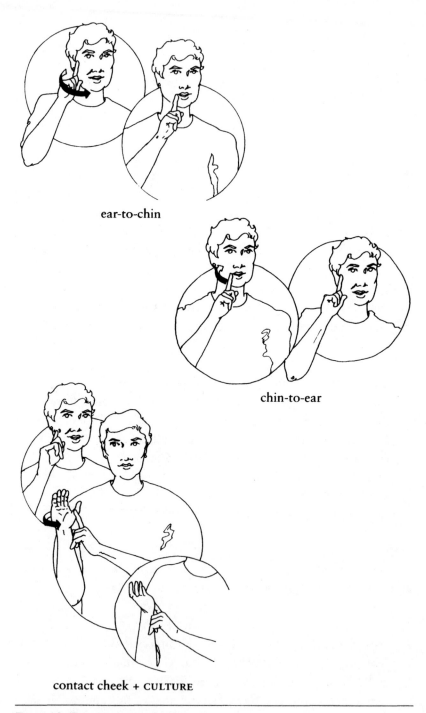

ear-to-chin

chin-to-ear

contact cheek + CULTURE

Figure 10. Three variants of DEAF

compound signs, such as DEAF⌢CULTURE, DEAF⌢INSTITUTION, DEAF⌢WORLD, and DEAF⌢WAY.

2. The location of the preceding sign: We wanted to see whether the location of the preceding sign had any effect on the location of DEAF, so we noted whether the preceding sign was produced at the ear or above ("high," as in FATHER), between the ear and the chin ("middle," as in KID), or at the chin or below ("low," as in PRIDE). We also noted whether DEAF was preceded just by a pause, that is, without a sign.

3. The location of the following sign: We also wanted to see whether the location of the following sign had any effect on the location of DEAF, so we noted where the following sign was produced, just as we did with the preceding sign.

4. Our videotapes show people mostly just chatting but sometimes also telling stories, so we wanted to see whether that would make a difference in the location of DEAF. Thus we noted whether DEAF occurred in a conversation or a story.

Overall we found that people use many more noncitation than citation forms of DEAF. In fact, six groups of signers used noncitation forms more than 90 percent of the time. Older signers in Virginia, for example, used noncitation forms 96 percent of the time. Only three groups of signers—young people in Maryland and signers over twenty-five in Massachusetts—used the citation form for the majority of tokens of DEAF: It seems that in ASL, as in other languages, people use the language the way they want to use it, regardless of what may be written in dictionaries.

When we analyzed the factors that influence people's choice of the citation form of DEAF or one of the noncitation forms, we found that the most important constraint is the grammatical function of the sign. When DEAF is a predicate, it is signed ear-to-chin more often than when it serves some other grammatical function. When it is in a compound, it tends to be contact-cheek. Nouns and adjectives are both ear-to-chin and chin-to-ear. Chin-to-ear and contact-cheek also tend to occur in stories, while ear to chin occurs slightly more often in regular conversation. The location of the preceding and following sign has no effect on the choice between the citation form and a noncitation form. When comparing the two noncitation forms—chin-to-ear and contact-cheek—the grammatical function is still the most important factor, with contact-cheek occurring most often in compound signs. In addition, we found that the location of the following sign is also important. The contact-cheek form of DEAF occurs more frequently when the next sign is at the ear or above or at the chin or below, but not when the following sign is on the cheek. Charts 1 and 2 contain a quick summary of our findings.

We had expected to find that the location of the preceding and following signs plays a big role in the variation of DEAF, but, surprisingly, the grammatical function of DEAF itself turns out to have the most influence. For the social factors, we found that DEAF also exhibits **sociolinguistic** patterning, but only age and region appear to be important. Other factors such as ethnicity, gender, language background, and social class are not significant. Age and region have a complicated relationship. For example, the Boston signers in general use the ear-to-chin form more often than the chin-to-ear or contact-cheek forms, and the older signers are more likely to use ear-to-chin than the middle aged or young signers. In Maryland we see the opposite: The youngest signers are most likely to use the ear-to-chin form. In Virginia, California, and Washington state, the younger signers tend to use the chin-to-ear and contact-cheek forms. In California, Louisiana, Virginia, and Washington, the middle-aged group consistently tends to use the ear-to-chin forms more often than the oldest and youngest signers in these areas. We think that this may be because the signers in the middle group were in school at the time when ASL was beginning to be recognized as a real language and when linguists were starting to do research on ASL and other sign languages. These signers may have a heightened awareness of what is considered the "correct" form (ear-to-chin) and thus use it more.

LOCATION SIGNS

We looked at 2,594 examples of signs that are signed at the forehead in citation form but can move down. For convenience, we refer to signs in this class as "location signs," that is, signs that may vary in their location.

Chart 1. Linguistic Influences on the Choice of a Form of DEAF: Ear-to-Chin vs. Chin-to-Ear or Contact-Cheek

DEAF, ear-to-chin vs. chin-to-ear or contact-cheek

Overall	Noncitation forms (69%) are far more common than citation forms (31%).
Grammatical function	Compound signs tend to be contact-cheek or chin-to-ear.
	Predicates tend to be ear-to-chin.
	Nouns may be any of the three, but the ear-to-chin form is the most common.
Conversation or story	Stories tend to be chin-to-ear or contact-cheek.
	Conversation tends to have more ear-to-chin than stories do.

Chart 2. Linguistic Influences on the Choice of a Form of DEAF (Chin-to-Ear vs. Contact-Cheek)

DEAF, chin-to-ear vs. contact-cheek

Overall	Contact-cheek is found in all grammatical categories but occurs much less frequently in nouns (17%), adjectives (10%), and predicates (17%) than in compounds (56%).
Grammatical function	Compound signs tend to be contact-cheek.
	Predicates, nouns, and adjectives tend to be chin-to-ear.
Location of following sign	Low and high signs are often preceded by contact-cheek.
	Middle and pause are usually preceded by chin-to-ear.

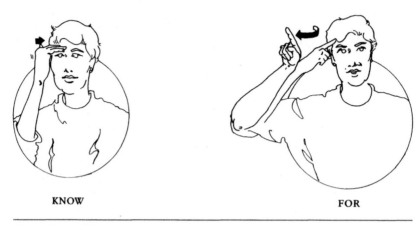

Figure 11. Citation forms of KNOW and FOR

Examples of location signs are verbs such as KNOW, BELIEVE, and REMEMBER, adjectives such as FEDERAL and DIZZY, nouns such as DEER and FATHER, prepositions such as FOR, and interrogatives such as WHY. Figure 11 shows KNOW and FOR in their citation forms, while Figure 12 shows them at lower locations.

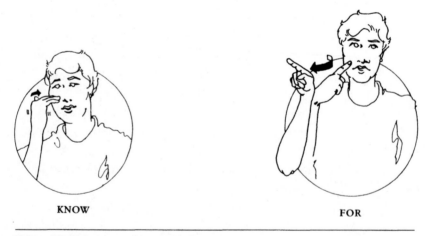

Figure 12. Noncitation forms of KNOW and FOR

⊙

Clip 6. The CD shows three examples of location signs: (1) The man signs PRO.1 ("I") THINK and then several other signs (WONDER, BOY, KNOW, KNOW-NOTHING), all at the forehead level; (2) the woman on the right signs SEARCH in neutral space, not in front of her face; and (3) the girl in the middle signs KNOW, meaning "You know?" very low on her cheek.

⊙

As with DEAF, we looked at each example and noted important things:

- **the grammatical function of the sign:** As we mentioned earlier, the signs in this group can be verbs, adjectives, nouns, prepositions, and interrogatives.
- **the preceding sign and following sign:** We noted whether a sign preceded or followed the location sign or whether a pause was there. We also noted whether the location of the preceding sign and following sign was at the level of the signer's head or at the level of the signer's body (at the neck or below). Then we noted whether the preceding or following sign made contact with the body.

As with DEAF, we noted whether the location sign occurred in a conversation or in a story. And once again, as with DEAF, we found that the grammatical category of the sign is the most important influence on the variation. As Chart 3 illustrates, prepositions and interrogative words tend to be lowered, whereas nouns, verbs, and adjectives are more likely to be produced at the forehead level.

Moreover, characteristics of the preceding and following signs play a role: Both the preceding location and the following contact are important. We found that if the preceding sign is produced at the head level, the location sign tends to be produced there, too. If the preceding sign is produced below the neck, the location sign tends to be lowered. If the following sign has no contact with the body, the location sign tends to be

Chart 3. Linguistic Influences on the Location of Signs such as KNOW

Linguistic influence	Finding
Overall	Noncitation (lowered) forms are slightly more common (53%) than citation forms (47%).
Grammatical function	Prepositions are more likely to be signed lower than the citation form (59%). Nouns and verbs are neutral (52%). The relatively few adjectives in the study are likely to be produced in citation form (65%).
Location of the preceding sign	When the preceding sign is produced at the level of the body, signs such as KNOW are slightly more likely be produced lower than the citation form (53%) than when the preceding sign is produced at the level of the head (48%).
Contact of the following sign with the body	When the following sign has no contact with the body, signers are more likely to choose a lowered form (55%) than when the following sign contacts the body (48%).

lowered, whereas if the following sign makes contact with the body, the location sign tends to be produced at the forehead level.

As Chart 4 shows, the signs that vary in location show sociolinguistic patterning similar to DEAF. Many of the social factors are significant. For example, the younger signers produced the signs below the forehead more than did the signers in the middle aged and older groups. Men tended to lower the signs more than women. This result parallels variation in spoken languages, in which women consistently use more citation forms than men do. Participants from Deaf ASL-signing families are slightly more

Chart 4. Social Influences on the Location of Signs Like KNOW

Social influence	Finding
Age	Signers over 55 are more likely to use the citation form; and younger signers are more likely to use the noncitation form.
Gender	Males use more noncitation forms than females.
Region	Signers in California, Louisiana, Maryland, Massachusetts, Missouri, and Kansas are more likely to use noncitation forms than signers in Washington or Virginia.
Language background	Children of Deaf parents are less likely to use noncitation forms than children of hearing parents.
Ethnicity and social class	Middle- and working-class Caucasian signers are more likely to use noncitation forms than African American signers. Working-class, African American signers are the least likely to use noncitation forms.

likely to produce the forehead-level citation forms, whereas participants from nonsigning families produce slightly more lowered forms. African American signers prefer the citation forms produced at the forehead level, whereas white signers produce more lowered forms. Finally, participants from the more rural sites that we visited—Frederick, Staunton, and Bellingham—also prefer the forehead forms.

SIGNS WITH A 1 HANDSHAPE

The videotapes show many examples of signs with a 1 handshape. Very often a sign that has a 1 handshape in a sign language dictionary is produced with an L handshape, a 5 handshape, or some other handshape.

For example, in the phrase PRO.1 PREFER ("I prefer"), the sign PREFER has an Open 8 handshape, and it is not uncommon for the PRO.1 sign also to have this handshape. When someone signs PRO.1 KNOW ("I know"), the handshape of the PRO.1 often changes to look like the Bent B of KNOW.

⊙

Clip 7. The CD shows four examples of 1 handshape signs: (1) The young man signs PRO.1 ("I") DON'T-KNOW WHY, and the handshape of the PRO.1 resembles that of DON'T-KNOW; (2) the man on the right of the sofa signs PRO.1 ("I") CAN'T REMEMBER with a standard handshape PRO.1; (3) the man on the right signs PRO.1 OPEN-MOUTH, SHAKE-HEAD, with the standard handshape for PRO.1; and (4) the man on the far right signs PRO.1 ("I") LOOK-AT, with a PRO.1 handshape very much like the handshape for LOOK-AT.

⊙

We looked at more than five thousand examples of signs with 1 handshapes. The three most common variants account for approximately 95 percent of the examples: the citation 1 handshape (index finger extended, all other fingers and thumb closed); the L handshape (thumb and index extended, all other fingers closed); and the 5 handshape (all fingers open). These are illustrated in Figure 13.

Figure 13. Variants of 1 handshape signs

As with DEAF and the location of signs such as KNOW, we noted a number of important potential influences on the way the signs are produced:

- **the grammatical function of the sign:** Signs that use the 1 handshape can be pronouns ("I," "you," "he," etc.), wh-words (WHERE, WHEN), grammatical function words (FOR), adverbs (REALLY), verbs (GO, CANCEL), adjectives (BLACK, LONG), and nouns (WEEK, MONTH).
- **the preceding sign and the following sign:** We took note of the handshape of the preceding and following signs: whether the thumb was extended, whether fingers other than the index were extended, and whether the index was straight or hooked.
- **context:** As with DEAF and the location signs, we noted whether the sign occurred in a conversation or in a story.

Charts 5 and 6 summarize what we found.

As with DEAF and the location signs, the grammatical function of the 1 handshape signs plays the most important role in the variation. Signers prefer the citation form for nouns, adjectives, verbs, adverbs, grammatical function words, wh-words, and pronouns in the third person ("she," "he"). This preference is stronger for some grammatical classes such as nouns and adjectives than for others, such as PRO.3. For second-person pronouns ("you") and first-person pronouns ("I"), signers prefer the L or 5 handshape. In addition, the handshapes of the surrounding signs influence the variation. For example, if the thumb was extended in the preceding sign, the sign we were focusing on was more likely to be an L or a 5.

Since we were looking at three different variants (1, L, and 5), we did many analyses. All of the social factors of age, social class, ethnicity, region, and language background were significant in at least one analysis. For example, signers aged 26–54, working-class signers, African American signers, and signers from Massachusetts, California, Kansas/Missouri, and Louisiana slightly prefer the citation form (1), whereas younger and older signers, middle-class signers, Caucasian signers, and signers from Maryland, Washington, and Virginia tend to use the L or 5 forms.

Chart 5. Linguistic Influences on the Choice of a 1 Handshape Sign

Linguistic influence	Citation form (one hand)	Noncitation form 1 (L handshape)	Noncitation form 2 (open hand)
Grammatical category	Nouns, adjectives, verbs, grammatical function signs, wh-signs, and PRO.3 favor. PRO.2 slightly and PRO.1 strongly disfavor.	Wh-signs and pronouns favor. Nouns, adjectives, verbs, and adverbs disfavor; grammatical function signs are neutral.	PRO.1 strongly favors; PRO.2 is neutral. Signs of all other categories disfavor.
Preceding thumb	Closed thumb favors.	Open thumb favors.	Open thumb favors.
Preceding fingers	Closed fingers favor.	Closed fingers favor.	Open fingers favor.
Preceding index	Straight index favors.	No significant effect.	No significant effect.
Following thumb	Closed thumb favors.	Open thumb favors.	Open thumb favors.
Following fingers	Closed fingers favor.	Closed fingers favor.	Open fingers favor.
Overall	The citation form is the most common (40%), followed by the L handshape (30%), and the open-hand form (25%).		

Chart 6. Social Influences on the Choice of a 1 Handshape Sign

Social influence	Citation form (one hand)	Noncitation form 1 (L handshape)	Noncitation form 2 (open hand)
Age	Older and younger signers favor; middle group disfavors.	Older signers favor; younger and middle groups disfavor.	Older and middle groups favor; younger groups disfavors.
Social class	Working-class signers favor slightly; middle-class signers disfavor.	No significant effect.	No significant effect.
Region	California, Kansas/Missouri Massachusetts, and Louisiana favor; Maryland, Washington and Virginia disfavor.	Maryland, Washington and Virginia favor; California, Kansas/Missouri, Massachusetts, and Louisiana favor.	Maryland, Washington and Virginia favor; California, Kansas/Missouri, Massachusetts, and Louisiana favor.
Language background	No significant effect.	No significant effect.	Signers from Deaf families disfavor; signers from hearing families favor.

We see from this that, as in spoken languages, ASL has patterned phonological variation that correlates with social factors. Some of these social factors, such as age and language background, behave uniquely in the Deaf community.

DISCUSSION QUESTIONS

1. List as many signs as you can that show variation in hand-shape, location, palm orientation, or movement.
2. List other social factors that you think may play a role in variation in ASL and discuss their role.

5

Syntactic Variation

In the variation section, we noted that variation can occur not only in the parts of signs but also in the arrangement of word-sized units. When the parts of sentences can vary, then, we are seeing *syntactic variation*. To analyze this we looked at stories that the participants told during the free conversation. Often when people are chatting, one person will tell others a story related to the topic they are discussing; some of these stories are relatively long, while others are short. Stories are good to analyze because it is easy to see where they begin and end. We looked at stories from all seven regions, from men and women, from middle-class and working-class signers, and from African American and Caucasian signers.

⊙

Clip 8. The concepts discussed here are also covered in the Syntactic Variation section of the CD. Specific examples in this clip are repeated in other clips refered to in this chapter.

⊙

ASL has different kinds of verbs. In some verbs, such as GIVE and TEASE, the location and the palm orientation tell who the first person ("I") is and who the second ("you") or third ("he" or "she") person is. For example, in the sentence PRO.1 GIVE PRO.2 ("I give you"), the hand moves from near the signer's body to the space in front of the signer. In the sentence PRO.2 GIVE PRO.1 ("You give me"), the hand moves in toward the signer. Even though signers sometimes sign separate signs for PRO.1 and PRO.2, verbs such as GIVE and TEASE, called *indicating verbs* do not require these separate signs.[6] But other verbs, such as THINK, FEEL, and KNOW, do not have anything in their orientation or location that indicates first, second, or third person. These *plain* verbs require signers to produce separate signs for the subject and object, as in PRO.1 THINK ("I think").[7] But these verbs often occur without a sign for first, second, or third person, and we wanted to understand why.

⊙

Clip 9. In the video example we see three examples of sentences with pronouns: (1) The older man signs #DR #BRILL (PRO.2) KNOW PRO.3 ("him")? The parentheses around PRO.2 indicate that he does not actually sign PRO.2 ("you"); (2) the man is quoting a woman and signs (PRO.1) FEEL NERVOUS. Again, the parentheses indicate that he does not actually produce the sign PRO.1 ("I"); (3) the man in the middle signs (PRO.1) HAVE SON NOW, (PRO.1) HAVE SON. He does not actually sign PRO.1.

⊙

In the stories, we looked at each sentence that had a plain verb and noted whether it had a pronoun subject. We also noted some other things about each sentence:

1. Same or switch reference: In the two sentences "I just stood there. I was quiet," the pronouns refer to the same person; this is called "same reference." But in the two sentences "He just stood there. I was quiet," the reference switches from "he" in the first sentence to "I" in the second. We expected the pronouns to be left out more in same-reference situations.

2. Person and number: We noted whether the reference was to first-person singular ("I"), second-person singular ("you"), third-person singular (he" or "she"), first-person plural ("we"), and second- or third-person plural ("you" or "they").

3. Sentence type: We noted what kind of sentence it was—declarative, yes/no question, wh-question, and so forth.
4. Constructed dialogue and constructed action: This is what people commonly know as "taking a role," and it happens very often in ASL conversations. Signers show what someone else signed or what they did. We noted whether the sentence was part of constructed dialogue or action.
5. English influence: Signers often use signs and structures that show the influence of spoken or written English. For example, one participant signed LIZARD I-S #BACK HOME, fingerspelling the English word "is." Another participant signed ANYWAY PRO.1PL GET HOME ("Anyway, we got home"), using the English construction "to get home." We noted whether the sentence showed this kind of influence from English.

We analyzed 429 sentences from nineteen different stories. We include one of the stories here, told by a teacher in Kansas, which describes the reactions of students and the teacher in an interpreter training class to the bombing of the Oklahoma City federal building in 1995. You will have noticed that the following transcription does not look exactly like written English. Linguists use transcriptions to help them represent and analyze ASL. Here are some transcription conventions: (1) Signs are represented with small capital letters called *glosses;* (2) words such as index-location represent pointing; (3) full fingerspelling (in which each letter is clear) is represented by dashes, for example, O-K-A-C-I-T-Y; (4) fingerspelling that is more like a sign is marked with this symbol: #, as in #THEN; (5) repetition of a sign is shown with +, as in CRY++; (6) glosses do not include verb and noun markings in the same way these words would be written in English, for example, TWO STUDENT vs. "two students"; (7) CL: stands for classifier; (8) "rs" stands for role shift; and (9) POSS stands for possessive ("my").

AWFUL! PRO.1 THINK-OF-SOMETHING. POSS.1 CLASS index-location. PRO.1 TEACH INTERPRET TRAIN PROGRAM index-location. HAVE TWO STUDENT FROM O-K-A C-I-T-Y index-location. THAT EXACTLY ONE WEEK (false start)—BOMB ONE WEEK LATER (headnod). ANNOUNCE HAVE TIME

NINE-O'CLOCK index-location SILENCE FOR ONE MINUTE. FINE. DURING
POSS.1 CLASS TIME EIGHT T-(O) TEN. FINE. RESPECT PRO.1 (false start) (rs:
PRO.3). PRO.3 WANT HONOR. FINE. WELL GET-UP (CL: people standing in
a semicircle). BE-QUIET. STAND. BE-QUIET. (pause) (gesture) #THEN FEW
MINUTE PRO.1 OPEN-EYES. THINK ENOUGH TIME. FINISH PRO.1 (CL: eyes
look up). (rs: be startled). HOLD-IT. SILLY! STUDENT CRY+++. LOOK-AT.
WOW TOUCH-HEART (rs: index-location). FIND POSS.3 SEVERAL FRIENDS
DIE index-location TOO. S-O PRO.3 KNOW SOME PEOPLE index-location.
WOW LOOK-AT WONDER TOUCH-HEART WOW.

(How awful! That makes me think of something that happened in the
class I teach over in the interpreter training program. There are two students in it from Oklahoma City. This was exactly one week—this was one
week after the bombing. It was announced that there would be a moment
of silence at nine o'clock. No problem. It would be during my class
(which runs from eight to ten o'clock). It's important to have a time to
pay respect, and that's what the students wanted to do. So we all got up.
We were completely silent. We just stood there and kept quiet. After a few
minutes I opened my eyes. I thought enough time had gone by, but when
I looked up I saw how wrong I was! One of the students was really cry-
ing. Wow—that sure got to me. It turned out she'd had friends who died
there. So she actually knew people involved. Wow, I couldn't imagine how
she felt. Seeing that was really moving.)

The analysis of pronoun use in stories such as the example given here
shows that the variation is systematic. Signers used a pronoun with only
35 percent of the plain verbs. English influence is the most important factor in the variation—that is, if a sentence had some English-like structure,
the signer was likely to produce the subject pronoun. Signers produced
more first-person pronouns ("I") than second- and third-person pronouns, both singular and plural. As we expected, pronouns tend to be left
out more in same-reference situations and to be produced more in switch-
reference ones, although even with the subject changes, signers omitted
the pronoun slightly more than half the time. Older signers and women
tend to produce pronouns more than middle-aged and younger signers

Chart 7. Linguistic and Social Influences on Signers' Pronoun Use

Influence	Finding
English influence	Favors pronoun use.
Person and number	First-person singular favors pronoun use; all others disfavor.
Subject continuity (same subject as preceding clause)	Different subject favors pronoun use; same subject disfavors pronoun use.
Constructed action ("taking the role")	Constructed action disfavors pronoun use.
Age	Older signers (55+) favor pronoun use; signers 15–54 disfavor pronoun use.
Gender	Women use more pronouns (41%) than men (29%).
Overall	In the majority of sentences (65%), pronouns are omitted.

and men. Finally, pronouns tended to show up less in "taking the role" situations. Chart 7 summarizes the linguistic and social influences on signers' use of pronouns.

DISCUSSION QUESTIONS

1. Can you think of other examples of variation in ASL sentence structure? For example, can some signs be produced at both the beginning and the end of a sentence? Is there variation in facial expressions?

6

Lexical Variation

As we mentioned earlier, we selected two people from each group and showed them a set of thirty-four pictures and fingerspelled words to see which signs they would produce for the objects and actions shown. We chose the stimuli based on earlier work on variation in ASL and also included some that reflect recent changes in technology and country names (see Figure 14).[8]

Before we talk about what we found, we need to talk a little bit more about two kinds of lexical variation. One has to do with signs for a concept that are completely different from one another, signs that share no formal characteristics. We see this in the various signs for PIZZA: Some variants are fingerspelled, while others are representative of a person taking a bite out of a piece of pizza or of the round plate on which pizza is served. These *separate variants* do not share handshapes, locations, palm orientation, or movement. They can be seen in Figure 15.

⊙

Clip 10. The concepts discussed here are also covered in the Lexical Variation section of the CD. Specific examples in this clip are repeated in other clips referred to in this chapter.

⊙

Another kind of lexical variation occurs when a concept may be represented by a number of signs that are all clearly related in some way. Figure 16, which shows different signs for BANANA, illustrates this. We see that the base hand is a 1 handshape and that the active hand moves down

AFRICA	COMPUTER	MICROWAVE	SANDWICH
ARREST	DEER	MITTENS	SNOW
BANANA	DELICIOUS	PANTS (men's)	SOON
CAKE	DOG	PANTS (women's)	SQUIRREL
CANDY	EARLY	PERFUME	STEAL
CEREAL	FAINT	PIZZA	THIEF
CHEAT	FEAR	RABBIT	TOMATO
CHERRIES	GLOVES	RELAY	
CHICKEN	JAPAN	RUN	

Figure 14. The thirty-four stimuli

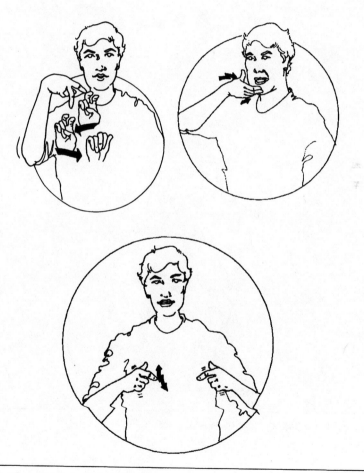

Figure 15. Lexical variants of PIZZA

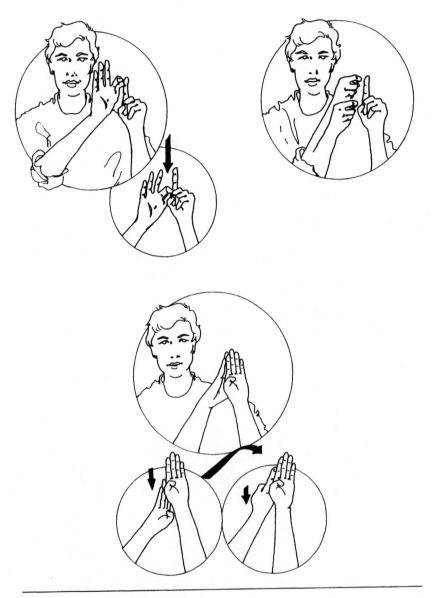

Figure 16. Lexical variants of BANANA

the sides of the base hand with a variety of different handshapes: F, A, 1, X, G, or V. These are *phonologically related variants.*

⊙

Clip 11. The CD shows a group from Maryland producing different forms of BANANA, while groups from Kansas and Boston show different forms of PIZZA.

⊙

We wanted to see how many separate variants and how many phonologically related variants there were for each of our stimuli. Figure 17 presents the stimuli again. The number next to each one represents the number of separate variants we found for each sign, including both phonological variants (different versions of the same sign) and different signs.

This shows that some signs have many separate variants whereas others have only a few. Participants produced only two separate signs for SNOW: One was a combination of the signs WHITE and SNOW (fingers in a 5 handshape, palm down, wiggling as they move down), sometimes produced without WHITE; in the other, the participants fingerspelled #SNOW and then signed it. EARLY had the most variants, thirteen, including an open 8 handshape moving across the back of the base hand, a 3 handshape on the forehead, as in ROOSTER, a two-handed sign with L handshapes moving out from the chest, and so on. And we saw the variants of PIZZA and BANANA shown in Figures 15 and 16.

⊙

Clip 12. The narrator shows different forms for EARLY and SNOW.

⊙

In all of these variants we noticed some very interesting things. One was that even though some of the signs had a lot of variants, for 27 of the 34 stimuli, one variant was shared across all of the seven regions. That

AFRICA	5	COMPUTER	5	MICROWAVE	6	SANDWICH	5
ARREST	11	DEER	4	MITTENS	5	SNOW	2
BANANA	5	DELICIOUS	4	PANTS (men's)	4	SOON	9
CAKE	4	DOG	3	PANTS (women's)	4	SQUIRREL	5
CANDY	6	EARLY	13	PERFUME	4	STEAL	2
CEREAL	11	FAINT	11	PIZZA	5	THIEF	3
CHEAT	11	FEAR	3	RABBIT	3	TOMATO	5
CHERRIES	5	GLOVES	2	RELAY	6		
CHICKEN	5	JAPAN	2	RUN	4		

Figure 17. The thirty-four stimuli with the number of separate variants

means that 79 percent of the signs have a shared variant across all of the sites. As part of the research for the project we looked at the history of the residential schools for deaf students at each of the seven sites. We found that the schools were commonly founded either by graduates of the American School for the Deaf (ASD) in Hartford, Connecticut, which was the first school for deaf students in America and was founded by Thomas Gallaudet and Laurent Clerc, or by graduates of other schools who were themselves educated by ASD graduates or instructors. Figure 18 illustrates what we found: a steady progression of ASL users from Hartford, Connecticut, all the way to Washington state. So it is not at all surprising to find some signs shared by all of the signers in our seven sites. And of course, the role of the schools is supplemented by the role played by sports, civic, and religious organizations in the deaf community, organizations that have always brought deaf people together from all over the country.

⊙

Clip 13. The narrator shows different forms of CHICKEN.

⊙

On the other hand, we also found that for 28 of the 34 signs, African American signers produced signs that the Caucasian signers did not. The

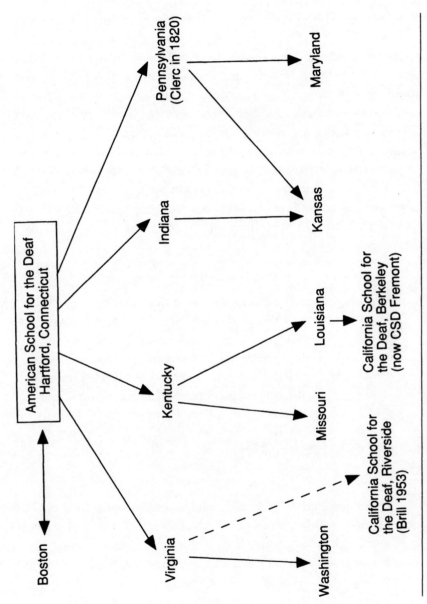

Figure 18. Links between the American School for the Deaf and the seven project sites

only signs for which the African American signers did not have their own variants are CAKE, MICROWAVE, JAPAN, SANDWICH, THIEF, and STEAL. And while the Caucasian signers had fingerspelled variants of ARREST, BANANA, FEAR, and GLOVES, the African Americans did not, but they did fingerspell DEER and RABBIT, which the Caucasian signers did not.

Earlier research on lexical variation shows that Caucasian signers tend to produce signs such as RABBIT on the head whereas African American signers tend to produce them on the hands and that African American signers produce the two-handed form of DEER more than the one-handed sign.[9] We found that both African American and Caucasian signers in all three age groups produced high and low forms of RABBIT and one- and two-handed forms of DEER. If a change is occurring, it is not completed yet.

⊙

Clip 14. A group from Louisiana shows their signs for TOMATO, RABBIT, and DEER. Although they all sign the low form of RABBIT, they show variation with TOMATO. The man signs it with two identical handshapes while the two women use two different handshapes. In addition, the man produces a one-handed version of DEER, while the women produce two-handed versions. Two young men from Kansas produce two forms of SNOW: The man on the right signs the compound form that includes WHITE, whereas the man on the left does not.

⊙

We see one kind of lexical variation in DEER and RABBIT and in signs such as SNOW, which can be signed with and without WHITE, and TOMATO, in which the two handshapes may be the same (both a 1 handshape) or different (the base hand is a flat O, and the active hand is a 1 handshape). This variation has to do with changes in some part of the sign: the handshape, the number of hands, or the location. This is different from what we see with signs such as JAPAN and AFRICA, where new signs have been introduced into ASL and are completely different from the existing

ASL signs. In the case of JAPAN, the Japanese Sign Language sign for the country has been borrowed into ASL. In the case of AFRICA, it seems that the newer sign, which outlines the continent, was proposed by someone during a formal lecture. The reasons for the introduction of the new signs for JAPAN and AFRICA are similar, having to do with showing respect for different cultures and getting away from any ASL signs considered to be racist because of their focus on physical characteristics. We found that all of the participants in the young and middle-aged group use the new signs, while some of the older signers still use the old signs.

⊙

Clip 15. Two men from Maryland produce an old sign and a new sign for AFRICA, and the one who produces the new sign briefly explains why. A group in Boston produces both the old and new signs for JAPAN.

⊙

DISCUSSION QUESTIONS

1. Go through the list of thirty-four signs and compare your signs to those of other people you know. How many variants for each sign do you find?
2. Which signs are used in your area for JAPAN and AFRICA? What about signs for other countries?
3. Are there differences in your area in the signs used by Caucasian, African American, Latino, and Asian signers? Describe the differences.

7

Collecting Variable Data

A book about sociolinguistic variation needs to spend some time talking about how to collect data. To study sociolinguistic variation, researchers aim to gather a lot of examples of natural language use and they also want those examples to be representative of the community that uses it.[10] Researchers face a number of issues, some of which present special problems for researchers studying sign languages.

One of these is the fact that we want to observe natural language use. However, when people know that their language is being observed, the language itself often changes—it may become more formal and less natural. A sociolinguist named William Labov called this the "Observer's Paradox."[11] That is, our goal is to analyze the language people use when they are not being recorded. However, the only way we can get good samples of language is by recording. Researchers working on spoken language variation typically record only the voice; the face of the participant cannot be seen. But researchers working on sign language variation have to use video cameras, and this means that it is impossible to preserve the anonymity of the participants. The researchers and other people will see the participants' faces. Because people may simply not want their faces shown in a relatively small community, it is often difficult to recruit participants in Deaf communities. To recruit people for the study, we relied on the assistance of contact people. These were well-respected members of the communities who were in contact with a lot of people. They recruited participants and explained to them the purpose and importance of the project.

For more than forty years we have known that socioeconomic status sometimes plays a role in variation in spoken languages—that is, working-class people may speak differently from middle-class people. Researchers have not studied in depth the role of socioeconomic status in sign language variation, and we cannot assume that the same labels that work for users of spoken languages also apply to sign language users. In our study we classified people by educational background and employment experience: Participants who attended the residential school and did not continue on for higher education, stayed in the area, and were employed in blue-collar, vocational jobs were considered working class; participants who attended the residential school, left for college and even higher degrees, had been back in the area for at least ten years, and were employed in white-collar jobs were considered middle class. Our classification worked fairly well, but future studies will no doubt expand on it.

As with socioeconomic status, spoken language studies have found that people from different ethnic groups speak differently—for example, systematic differences have been found between the speech of African Americans and Caucasians. The same no doubt holds true in Deaf communities. We saw this in the lexical differences discussed earlier. In this study we focus on African American and Caucasian signers, but future research needs to involve members of the Asian, Latino, and Native American Deaf communities, for example.

Studies of variation in spoken languages have always looked at speakers from different age groups, and age plays a role in sign language variation as well. But at least in the American Deaf community, researchers have to think about age along with the language policy of the schools deaf people attend. As we explained, older signers usually went to oral schools where sign language was prohibited, and middle-aged signers were in school when ASL was beginning to be recognized as a language and educators were beginning to use a method of signing and speaking at the same time. The youngest signers in our study are lucky to be attending bilingual programs in which ASL is used in the classroom. So the age groups in our study—15–25, 26–54, and 55 and up—reflect this relationship between age and school language policies.

The goal of the project called Sociolinguistic Variation in ASL was to provide a representative sample of ASL as it is used across the United States. For this project we settled on seven regions, all of which were chosen because they have thriving Deaf communities. There are of course many other thriving Deaf communities in the United States, and future studies can focus on these.

Finally, research on variation in sign languages must take into account the language background of the participants. While some ASL signers come from Deaf families who use ASL, many come from non-signing backgrounds, and as we saw with the location signs, this is a factor in the variation.

DISCUSSION QUESTIONS

1. What is the most interesting thing about variation for you?
2. Why is the study of variation important?

8

Summary and Conclusions

As you can see, ASL is just like other languages in having patterned variation that we can link to social factors, and some of these have to do specifically with Deaf communities. Even though both spoken and sign languages exhibit variation, the variation that sign languages exhibit is unique in some ways. A great deal of variation occurs in ASL, and in fact, we found many more noncitation forms than we did citation forms. Signers are more likely to sign DEAF from chin to ear, to lower the sign KNOW, and to sign PRO.1 ("I") with an L or a 5 handshape.

⊙

Clip 16. The narrator summarizes the conclusions.

⊙

We found the same kind of linguistic constraints that we see in spoken language variation, such as the influence of the sign before or after and the role of same or switch reference in pronoun variation. We also saw that the grammatical function of the variable sign is very important in sign language variation. We found, moreover, that the same kinds of social constraints that operate in spoken language variation—age, gender, region, and ethnicity—also operate in sign languages and that some unique social constraints are at work in sign language variation, such as whether a signer's parents are deaf ASL signers. Researchers have to consider age in connection with school language policies. In addition, any consideration of region has to take into account the way that ASL moved across the United States in the context of the residential schools for deaf students. We found lexical differences between African American and Caucasian signers, and we also learned that we need to consider certain special issues when collecting examples of variation in Deaf communities.

These materials are only a beginning. We hope that other researchers and signers will want to look at other variables in ASL and other varieties of ASL. Work on Tactile ASL, the variety of ASL that Deaf Blind signers use, for example, is showing us that Tactile ASL has some unique features.[12] Variation in the ASL that Hispanic, Asian, and Native American communities use and variation in other sign languages are open to further investigation as well.

Notes

1. Ceil Lucas, Robert Bayley, and Clayton Valli, *Sociolinguistic Variation in American Sign Language,* Sociolinguistics in Deaf Communities, vol. 7 (Washington, D.C.: Gallaudet University Press, 2001).

2. Clayton Valli and Ceil Lucas, *The Linguistics of American Sign Language,* 3d ed. (Washington, D.C.: Gallaudet University Press, 2001); R. Battison, *Lexical Borrowing in American Sign Language* (Silver Spring, Md.: Linstok, 1978); William O'Grady, Michael Dobrovolsky, and Mark Aronoff, *Contemporary Linguistics: An Introduction* (New York: St. Martin's, 1989).

3. Harlan Lane, *When the Mind Hears: A History of the Deaf* (New York: Random House, 1984); Harlan Lane, Robert Hoffmeister, and Ben Bahan, *Journey into the DEAF-WORLD* (San Diego: DawnSignPress, 1996); William C. Stokoe, Dorothy C. Casterline, and Carl G. Croneberg, *A Dictionary of American Sign Language on Linguistic Principles* (Washington, D.C.: Gallaudet College Press, 1965).

4. Scott Liddell and Robert E. Johnson, "American Sign Language: The Phonological Base," *Sign Language Studies* 64 (1989): 195–278.

5. Ibid.

6. Scott Liddell, "Indicating Verbs and Pronouns: Pointing Away from Agreement," in *The Signs of Language Revisited,* ed. Karen Emmorey and Harlan Lane (Mahwah, N.J.: Erlbaum, 2000), 303–20.

7. Carol Padden, *Interaction of Morphology and Syntax in American Sign Language* (New York: Garland, 1988).

8. James Woodward, "Some Observations on Sociolinguistic Variation and American Sign Language," *Kansas Journal of Sociology* 9, no. 2 (1973): 191–200; Edgar H. Shroyer and Susan Shroyer, *Signs across America* (Washington, D.C.: Gallaudet University Press, 1984).

9. James Woodward, "Black Southern Signing," *Language in Society* 5 (1976): 211–18; James Woodward and Susan De Santis, "Two to One

It Happens: Dynamic Phonology in Two Sign Languages," *Sign Language Studies* 17 (1977): 329–46.

10.   Gregory Guy, "The Quantitative Analysis of Linguistic Variation," in *American Dialect Research,* ed. Dennis R. Preston (Philadelphia: John Benjamins, 1993), 223–49.

11.   William Labov, *Sociolinguistic Patterns* (Philadelphia: University of Pennsylvania Press, 1972).

12.   Steven Collins and Karen Petronio, "What Happens in Tactile ASL?" in *Pinky Extension and Eye Gaze: Language Use in Deaf Communities,* ed. Ceil Lucas, Sociolinguistics in Deaf Communities, vol. 4 (Washington, D.C.: Gallaudet University Press, 1998), 18–37.

Supplementary Readings

The Importance of Variation Research for Deaf Communities

Ceil Lucas and Robert Bayley

We examine the importance of variation and other linguistic research for Deaf communities. Sociolinguistic variation in American Sign Language (ASL) was initially addressed by Carl Croneberg in the *Dictionary of American Sign Language (DASL)*, the first dictionary of a sign language based on linguistic principles (Stokoe, Casterline, and Croneberg 1965). This work was followed by studies of lexical, phonological, and grammatical variation. The treatment of variation in the *DASL* will be reviewed and research on variation described, with emphasis on the findings from a large-scale study of phonological variation. We will show that research on linguistic variation and other aspects of sign languages impacts Deaf communities in three ways.[1] First, the recognition that ASL exhibits sociolinguistic variation like other systems that we recognize as languages reinforces the hard-won status of ASL and other sign languages as real languages. Second, the study of variation in sign languages reinforces the position that systematic variation, or "orderly heterogeneity," is integral to the structure of all languages (Weinreich, Labov, and Herzog 1968). Understanding the nature of a language requires an understanding of variation. This in turn relates to the increasing awareness of modality differences between spoken and sign languages. Third, the findings from research on sign language structure and variation have had a direct impact on the educational and employment opportunities available to Deaf people.

This report was originally published in the *University of Pennsylvania Working Papers in Linguistics* 7(3): 175–89. The research reported here was supported by NSF Grants SBR #9310116 and SBR #9709522 to Gallaudet University. Clayton Valli, Mary Rose, Alyssa Wulf, Alison Jacoby, Leslie Saline, Susan Schatz, and Ruth Reed assisted with data collection, transcription, and coding.

PERSPECTIVES ON ASL

Users and observers of ASL have long been aware of variation in the language. Evidence can be seen in writings about deaf people's language use dating from the mid-nineteenth century. For example, at the fourth Convention of American Instructors of the Deaf in Staunton, Virginia, J. R. Keep described variation in the signs used by students at the school:

> there is a language of signs; a language having its own peculiar laws, and, like other languages, natural and native to those who know no other. . . . There may be different signs or motions for the same objects, yet all are intelligible and legitimate. . . . As a matter of fact, however, although the Deaf and Dumb, when they come to our public institutions, use signs differing in many respects from those in use in the institutions, yet they soon drop their peculiarities, and we have the spectacle of an entire community recalling objects by the same motions. (1857, 133)

In response to Keep's remarks, Harvey Peet referred to Deaf signers as "those to whom the language is vernacular" and added, "there is room for difference of dialects. One Deaf Mute may fall upon one sign and another upon another sign, for the same object, both natural" (1857, 144–46).

Despite the early awareness of variation indicated by comments such as those quoted above, formal research on variation in sign languages did not begin until the 1960s, with Croneberg's two appendices to the *DASL* (Stokoe et al. 1965). "The Linguistic Community" (Appendix C) describes the cultural and social aspects of the Deaf community and discusses economic status, patterns of social contact, and the factors that contribute to group cohesion, including the extensive personal and organizational networks that ensure frequent contact even among people who live on opposite sides of the country: "The deaf as a group have social ties with each other that extend farther across the nation than similar ties of perhaps any other American minority group" (Stokoe et al. 1965, 310).

Croneberg noted that these personal ties are reinforced by membership in organizations such as the National Association of the Deaf and the National Congress of the Jewish Deaf. These personal and organizational patterns of interaction are central to understanding language use and variation in ASL. While ASL is variable at a number of different linguistic levels, nevertheless Deaf people recognize a cohesive community of ASL users extending across the United States.

In "Sign Language Dialects" (Appendix D), Croneberg dealt with sociolinguistic variation, specifically as pertains to the preparation of a dictionary: "One of the problems that early confronts the lexicographers of a language is dialect, and this problem is particularly acute when the language has never before been written. They must try to determine whether an item in the language is standard, that is, used by the majority of a given population, or dialect, that is, used by a particular section of the population" (Stokoe et al. 1965, 313). He outlined the difference between what he termed *horizontal variation* (regional variation) and *vertical variation* (variation that occurs in the language of groups separated by social stratification) and stated that ASL exhibits both. He then described the results of a study of lexical variation undertaken in the southeast and New England. He found that for ASL, the state boundaries between North Carolina and Virginia also constituted dialect boundaries. North Carolina signs were not found in Virginia and vice versa. Maine, New Hampshire, and Vermont, however, exhibited less internal standardization, and state boundaries in New England tended to be much less important than in the South, with considerable overlap in lexical choice among the three states. He pointed out the key role of the residential schools in the dissemination of dialects: "At such a school, the young deaf learn ASL in the particular variety characteristic of the local region. The school is also a source of local innovations, for each school generation comes up with some new signs or modifications of old ones" (Stokoe et al. 1965, 314).

In his discussion of vertical variation, Croneberg mentioned the influence of age, ethnicity, gender, religion, and status. His definition of status encompassed economic level, occupation, relative leadership within the deaf community, and educational background. He also noted that professionally employed and financially prosperous graduates of Gallaudet College "tend to seek each other out and form a group. Frequently they use certain signs that are considered superior to the signs used locally. . . . Examples of such signs are Gallaudet signs, transmitted by one or more graduates of Gallaudet who are now teaching at a school for the deaf, and who are members of the local elite. The sign may or may not later be incorporated in the sign language of the local or regional community" (Stokoe et al. 1965, 318).

Finally, Croneberg commented on what a standard sign language might be and stated that "few have paid any attention to the term standard in the sense of 'statistically most frequent.' The tendency has been to divide sign language into good and bad" (Stokoe et al. 1965, 318), with older signers and educators of the deaf maintaining the superiority of their respective signs for various reasons. Croneberg neatly captured the essence of the difference between prescriptive and descriptive perspectives on language when he wrote, "What signs the deaf population actually uses and what certain individuals consider good signs are thus very often two completely different things" (1965, 319).

It is also useful to consider Croneberg's appendices within the context of other variation research that occurred at the same time. The 1960s and the 1970s were very busy for spoken languages and sign languages alike. Labov's study of vowel centralization on Martha's Vineyard was published in 1963, and his pivotal study of New York City speech followed in 1966. Both studies explored a new area, the correlation of linguistic variables with social factors. Shuy, Wolfram, and Riley completed their urban language study of Detroit in 1968, and Wolfram's dissertation on what is now known as African American Vernacular English appeared in 1969. Georgetown University established a doctoral program in sociolinguistics in 1971, and James Woodward, whose 1973 dissertation explored variation in a sign language, was among the first students. In short, the years immediately preceding and following the publication of the *DASL*, in which Croneberg's appendices appeared, were ones of growing awareness about sociolinguistics in general and variation in particular.

The years following the publication of the *DASL* witnessed a number of studies of variation in ASL. In addition to Woodward (1973), phonological variation in the form of thumb extension (e.g., FUNNY, BLACK) was explored by Battison, Markowicz, and Woodward (1975). Woodward, Erting, and Oliver (1976) looked at signs that are produced variably on the face or the hands (e.g., MOVIE, PEACH), and Woodward and DeSantis (1977) examined signs that are variably one-handed or two-handed. In a historical study, Frishberg (1975) looked at processes such as centralization still witnessed in ASL today. Morphological and syntactic variation have also been explored, as well as lexical variation. (For a full review of variation research in ASL, see Lucas, Bayley, and Valli 2001.)

THE IMPORTANCE OF VARIATION RESEARCH

Sign Languages as Real Languages

At the 1989 Deaf Way conference in Washington, D.C., Stokoe addressed the issue of why the publication of a new dictionary makes headline news. He wrote that a serious dictionary is much more than a word book. Using the example of the *Oxford English Dictionary,* he stated that "by defining hundreds of thousands of English words in phrases and sentences in English, it describes this language more completely than any other single book can do. . . . Between the covers of a serious dictionary we find, all ready for us, the tools of thought" (1994, 331). He dealt with the significance of the publication of sign language dictionaries, saying that beyond describing and arranging the tools of thought that sign language users need, a dictionary "can show the world that deaf signers can think in their sign languages, with logic and precision and even elegance. It can wipe out, as nothing else can so well, the false ideas that ignorant people have about deaf people and deaf society and sign languages" (332).

In discussing what guided him in the preparation of the *DASL* as early as 1957, Stokoe mentioned the thinking of George Trager and Henry Lee Smith: "They insisted that language could not be studied by itself . . . but must be looked at in direct connection to the people who used it, the things they used it to talk about, and the view of the world that using it imposed on them." (1994, 333) This perspective guided the inclusion of Croneberg's appendices in the *DASL,* appendices that showed "how language and culture as well as deafness formed a special community" (1994, 334). The recognition that ASL exhibits variation like other linguistic systems reinforces the status of ASL as a real language. And since it is known that variation is often the precursor to change, the study of variation in ASL, as in other languages, leads us to an understanding of how ASL changes.

The inclusion of information about variation in the *DASL*—that is, in a volume that by definition aims to represent the structure of a language and is accepted by the community as a reliable representation—also reinforces the position that rather than being just a curiosity or an anomaly, variation is an integral part of the structure of language and that in order to truly understand the nature of a language, variation must be considered. In this regard, in their pioneering work on variation, Weinreich et al. (1968) introduced the idea of structured heterogeneity as the most useful metaphor for understanding the nature of language: "The key to a rational conception of language change—indeed, of language itself—is the possibility of describing orderly differentiation in a language serving a community . . ." (99–100). The inclusion of information about variation in the *DASL* thus provides a much wider perspective on the fundamental nature of ASL structure, one that has led to an increasing awareness of modality differences between spoken languages and sign languages. These differences are evident in how variation is structured.

Systematic Variation in ASL

Our evidence for the structured nature of variation in ASL comes from a project that focused on phonological, syntactic, and lexical variation. The details of the project are described at length in Lucas et al. (2001). For the purposes of this report we will focus on the results of the analysis of phonological variation. We looked at the patterns of variation exhibited by three phonological variables: signs produced with a 1 handshape, the sign DEAF, and the location of a class of signs represented by i. The citation form (the form that appears in dictionaries and that is taught in sign language classes) for 1-handshape signs is index extended with all other fingers and the thumb closed. However, variation in 1-handshape signs may range from an extended thumb (the L handshape) to all fingers open (the open-hand variant). In citation form, the sign DEAF is produced from a location near the ear to a location near the chin, but also appears chin-to-ear and simply as a single contact of the finger on the cheek. Signs like KNOW are produced at the level of the forehead in citation form, but frequently move down to the cheek or even to the space in front of the signer. Multivariate analysis of more than 10,000 tokens showed that the variation exhibited by all three variables correlates with both linguistic and social factors. That all three variables exhibit significant correlations with both linguistic and social factors is not at all surprising. These kinds of correlations are characteristic of all human languages. What is unexpected, however, is the consistently strong role of grammatical factors in conditioning the patterning of the three variables.

Sociolinguistic research on spoken languages has shown that linguistic variables may be systematically conditioned by factors operating at different levels of the linguistic system. For example, numerous studies have shown that -t,d deletion in English is conditioned by the preceding and following phonological environments, stress, and the grammatical category of the word containing the cluster (e.g., Guy 1980). Although the fact that many sociolinguistic variables are constrained by factors operating at different linguistic levels may be a commonplace for students of spoken languages, phonological variation in ASL and other sign languages has heretofore been accounted for by positing phonological constraints alone, particularly the features of the preceding and/or following segments, without reference to structures other than the sequence of phonological segments.

The program of research on ASL until very recently has been to demonstrate that ASL, and by analogy other sign languages, are true languages. This work has proceeded by demonstrating that the structure of ASL parallels that of spoken languages and that its phonology and syntax are subject to the same kinds of processes that operate in spoken languages. In the process, this work has not considered the possibility that factors at different linguistic levels may constrain phonological variation. For example, Liddell and Johnson (1989) explain variation in all three of the variables discussed here—1 handshape, DEAF, the location of signs such as KNOW—exclusively by reference to features of the preceding and/or following segments.

The results of our analysis do not support Liddell and Johnson's claims. The core of our analysis of each variable involved identifying the linguistic factors that govern the observed variation. We hypothesized that features of the immediately preceding and following phonological environment would play key roles. For example, we assumed that the location of preceding and following signs would be important for understanding the variation in DEAF and in the location of signs such as KNOW. We assumed that the handshape of the preceding and following sign would play a role in the variation of 1-handshape signs. We therefore included factor groups consisting of the features of the preceding and following segments. However, Lucas's earlier analysis of DEAF (1995) had alerted us to the possible role played by grammatical function in explaining variation. That analysis, based on 486 tokens, found the syntactic category of the sign DEAF to be the only significant linguistic factor, with adjectives favoring noncitation forms, predicate adjectives slightly disfavoring them, and nouns strongly disfavoring them. Based on the results of Lucas (1995), in the larger study we included a factor group for the relevant grammatical categories of each variable along with the phonological and social factor groups. For DEAF, the grammatical categories included predicate adjective, noun, adjective, and adjective in a compound. For the location of signs such as KNOW, they included prepositions and interrogatives, nouns, verbs, and adjectives, and for 1-handshape signs, they included pronouns and lexical signs, the latter divided into nouns, adjectives, verbs, adverbs, and grammatical words. Table 1 summarizes the ranking of the factors for all three variables and shows that grammatical function is the most powerful factor in all three cases. This is a very surprising finding, with substantial implications. We will first discuss its

importance in terms of each variable and then offer a more global explanation that unifies all three variables.

The results for variation in 1-handshape signs show grammatical
function to be the first-order linguistic constraint on two of the three
main variants, +cf and open hand, and a significant constraint on the
third, L handshape. The 1-handshape findings suggest that conditioning
at the level of discourse structure and information packaging may be
more important for phonological variation in sign languages than previously thought. We can view the three variants as points on a continuum
of distance from the citation form: the citation form itself, a form in
which only the thumb is extended, and a class of forms in which other
fingers are also selected and extended. This continuum corresponds
inversely to a continuum of grammatical distance from the signing subject in the discourse setting: That is, the most salient referent in the discourse, the signer, is more likely to be referred to with a pronoun whose
form may vary maximally from the citation form. The addressee, also
salient in the discourse setting, is more likely to be referred to with a
pronominal form that diverges from the citation form only in features of
the thumb. Third-person referents, those not present in the setting, are
the most likely among the pronouns to be in citation form. In ASL pronouns, the indexical function is carried by the tips of the fingers, regardless of the handshape used. In nonindexical lexical signs, however, the
whole handshape carries part of the semantic load. The handshape in this
class is the most likely to be the citation form. Lexical signs may be produced as the L handshape variant, in which the thumb is also extended,
but they are less likely to take a handshape that is farther away from the
citation form than are pronouns, as this could convey a different meaning, or no meaning at all.

In the case of DEAF, the role of grammatical constraints in the choice
between a citation and noncitation form may represent a synchronic reflex
of a change in progress in which compounds are the most favorable environment for innovative forms, followed by nouns and adjectives and finally predicates. We also see both the chin-to-ear and contact-cheek forms
occurring with predicates, nouns, and adjectives. VARBRUL analysis

Table 1. Linguistic Constraints on Phonological Variation

Variable	Analysis	Constraint ranking
1 handshape	+cf vs. −cf	grammatical function > features of preceding and following handshapes (assimilation)
	L handshape vs. all others	features of preceding and following handshapes (assimilation) > grammatical function
	open hand vs. all others	grammatical function > features of preceding and following handshapes (assimilation)
DEAF	+cf vs. −cf	grammatical function > discourse genre
	chin-to-ear vs. contact-cheek	grammatical function > location of following segment (assimilation)
Location	+cf vs. −cf	grammatical function > contact with body of following sign > location of preceding sign

shows that when the citation (ear-to-chin) and noncitation forms (chin-to-ear and contact-cheek) of DEAF are compared, grammatical category is the main linguistic constraint on variation. These findings do not mean, however, that phonological factors never play a role. When we compare the noncitation forms to each other, grammatical function is still the most important factor, but the location of the following sign also plays a role, and we have evidence of assimilation: Following locations higher or lower than the usual location for the contact-cheek form slightly favor this form, while a following location at the contact-cheek location (as in the sign YES-TERDAY or GIRL) and a following pause both disfavor the contact-cheek form and favor the chin-to-ear form.

In the case of the lowering of signs such as KNOW, as with DEAF, grammatical function is the most important factor. Specifically, prepositions and interrogatives are most likely to be produced at a location lower than the temple. Nouns and verbs represent the neutral reference point. Adjectives favor the citation form. And the phonological factors of the location of the preceding sign and body contact in a following sign proved to be significant. So, the features of the preceding and following signs do play a role in variation, but their role is not as strong as grammatical category.

The analyses summarized here highlight several points. First, we cannot assume that only features of the preceding and/or following signs constrain phonological variation in sign languages. Indeed, the results of multivariate analyses show that is not the case (Lucas, Bayley, and Valli 2001). Second, just as with spoken languages, studies of variation in sign languages must be based on large amounts of data collected from representative samples of the language community. With all three phonological variables that we examined, we saw that while it might seem reasonable to assume that most important factors governing variation have to do with features of the preceding and following segments, this assumption is not always reliable. When examined in light of the actual language produced by real people, the claims and assumptions about all three variables could not be supported. Third, the consistent pattern observed across all three phonological variables examined here may help us sort out the types of constraints that may be unique to signed languages, e.g., indexicality, and those that are common to all languages, whether spoken or signed.

We have strong evidence, then, that grammatical constraints play a more important role than the features of the preceding and following signs in conditioning phonological variation in ASL. The challenge is to understand why this is so. The first answer is that, as in spoken languages, phonological variation in ASL is not constrained only by phonological factors. The focus heretofore may have been on features of the preceding and following signs, but large data- based quantitative studies such as ours show that grammatical factors must also be considered. A second answer leads to consideration of fundamental differences between spoken and sign languages. That sign languages are "real" languages, viable linguistic systems independent from the spoken languages with which they may coexist, has been amply demonstrated. However, having established that sign languages are languages, research on all aspects of sign language structure has begun to reveal some very fundamental and most likely modality-related differences between spoken and sign languages. Of most relevance here are the fundamental differences in how morphology functions and how these differences manifest themselves in variation. In many of the spoken languages in which phonological variation has been explored, morphology is a "boundary phenomenon." That is, meaningful units are added to the beginning or to the end of other units in the language in the form of plural markers, person and tense markers, derivational affixes and so forth. These units are added to an existing phonological environment. It stands to reason that when variation occurs, the immediate environment to which the units have been added is a good place to look for the basis of the variation. And in fact, many studies of spoken language variation have demonstrated the key role of the immediate phonological environment in governing variation.

However, morphology in sign languages is by and large not a boundary phenomenon. Very few affixes exist. Morphological distinctions are accomplished by altering one or more features in the articulatory bundle that makes up a hold or a movement segment or by altering the movement path of the sign. That is, segments are not usually added to other segments to provide information about, for example, person or aspect. Rather, the location feature of a segment (e.g., near the signer or away from the signer) indicates person, and movement between locations indicates subject and object of the verb; similarly, a particular movement path indicates continuative aspect or inceptive aspect (Emmorey 1999).

Based on the results of our analyses, it would seem that these fundamental differences manifest themselves in the variable components of the language. That is, the immediate phonological environment turns out not to have the major role in governing phonological variables, in part because the variables are not affixes. The grammatical category to which a variable belongs is consistently the first-order linguistic constraint. We suggest that, as the modality differences between spoken and signed languages manifest themselves in the basic phonological, morphological, and syntactic components of the language, so do they manifest themselves in the variation found in the language. As phonological and morphological processes go, so apparently goes variation.

The question arises as to the parallels between ASL and spoken languages such as Chinese that do not use affixes to any great extent. The question is difficult to answer. Although numerous studies of Chinese dialects exist, relatively few studies of Chinese employ variationist methods, and only Bourgerie's (1990) dissertation on sociolinguistic variation in Hong Kong Cantonese considers the effect of grammatical class on phonological variation.

We suggest, then, that the difference in modality may result in differences in the relative importance of the constraints. In the phonological variation observed thus far in sign languages, grammatical constraints are consistently more important than phonological ones. Ironically, it may be the visual nature of sign languages that reinforces the impressions and hypotheses that phonological variation in sign languages is governed only by constraints having to do with the features of the preceding and/or following segments. That is, we can actually see the lower and higher locations that precede and follow the sign DEAF and signs such as KNOW; we can see the handshapes that precede and follow 1 handshape signs. Being able to see the phonological environment surrounding the variation easily leads to hypotheses about this environment accounting fully for the variation. But these hypotheses are not supported by our data.

Finally, as suggested by the finding that the grammatical category to which a sign belongs is consistently the strongest constraint on variation, the study of variation in sign languages has important contributions to make to sociolinguistics in general. Having established that sign languages are fully functional languages, sign language researchers are now in a position to ask how studies of sign languages can help to expand our understanding of human language, an area in which Deaf scholars have an important role to play.

THE IMPORTANCE OF VARIATION RESEARCH FOR DEAF LIVES

In 1989 Stokoe stated that public attitudes toward deafness and deaf people and their sign language had changed, in part because of the publication of the *DASL*. Speaking of the changed attitudes demonstrated by the student-led campaign for a Deaf president of Gallaudet University, the nation's only university devoted primarily to the education of Deaf students, he commented: "I would like to think anyway—when the student leaders stood in front of TV cameras in March of 1988 and said that the University needed a deaf president now because the language and culture of deaf people must be respected—that the germ of that idea was presented in the dictionary twenty-three years earlier. . . . Owing in part, at least, to . . . a *Dictionary of American Sign Language,* there are now deaf men and women engaged in studying sign language and the culture of deaf communities" (1994, 334).

Others have made similar observations. George Detmold stated that he thought that the significance of the *DASL* "was that their [people's] language was treated here like any other language . . ." (cited in Maher 1996, 90). Mervin Garretson, former president of the National Association of the Deaf, stated in a volume of essays dedicated to Stokoe that "to know, once and for all, that our 'primitive' and 'ideographic gestures' are really a formal language on a par with all other languages of the world is a step towards pride and liberation" (Baker and Battison 1980, vi). The significance here comes not only from research on variation but from research on sign languages, of which variation is a part. This research has directly influenced the opportunities available to Deaf people in three areas: education, employment, and services.

Research on sign languages has led to the legitimization of sign languages and allowed for the discussion of what the medium of instruction should be in deaf education. Deaf people and educators now ask why it should not simply be sign language, a question that has to be understood within the historical context of deaf education. The history of deaf education is by now well documented, starting with the founding by Thomas Hopkins Gallaudet of the American School for the Deaf (formerly the American Asylum for the Deaf and Dumb) in 1817 in Hartford, Connecticut. Gallaudet was aided by Laurent Clerc, a French Deaf man who brought with him from France his knowledge of French Sign Language. Sign language was the medium of instruction at the American School, and, by 1826, there were 26 residential schools for the deaf in the United States, many founded by graduates of the American School and all using ASL as the medium of instruction. However, the tide of oralism began to rise in the 1870s, and by the 1880 conference of educators of the deaf held in Milan, Italy, sign language was seen as harmful to the development of deaf children. One of the slogans of the conference was "il gesto uccide la parola" ("gesture kills the word"). In the following decades, oralism rapidly gained the upper hand, and by 1907 there were 139 schools for the deaf and none used ASL (Lane, Hoffmeister, and Bahan 1996). This decline in ASL as the medium of instruction had direct consequences for deaf people employed as teachers. Prior to 1880, about 42 percent of teachers in residential schools were deaf; by the turn of the century, only 17 percent were deaf; and by 1996, only 7 percent were deaf.

The suppression of sign language, then, had a devastating impact on the lives of Deaf people in the late-nineteenth and early-twentieth centuries, both in terms of the language used for their education and their employment as teachers. The recognition of sign languages as real languages and linguistic research on sign languages since the 1960s has slowly begun to reverse the situation. Not only has the research helped to empower Deaf people all over the world, but it has allowed for the discussion of sign language as the medium of instruction in deaf education. Some schools in the United States and other countries such as Sweden, Venezuela, and Italy have implemented bilingual programs with instruction in the native sign language of the community and literacy in the majority written language. For some deaf students, these developments have led to the "unlocking of the curriculum" (Johnson, Liddell, and Erting 1989), that is, the provision of access to the academic content through a language that deaf students can understand, i.e., sign language. It has made for a slow increase in the number of deaf teachers. For example, the Gallaudet University graduate education program was established in 1891, but the first deaf student was not admitted until 1951. In fact, in 1890, Edward Miner Gallaudet, son of Thomas Hopkins and president of what was then Gallaudet College, commented on a conversation with Alexander Graham Bell, a leading proponent of oralism: "I told him plainly that he was entirely mistaken in this idea, that no deaf persons would be admitted to our normal [training] and that all its members would be thoroughly trained in the oral method for teaching the deaf" (cited in Jones and Achtzehn 1992, 4). As of this writing, the graduate education program averages about 100 students, 15 to 25 of whom are Deaf.

Research on sign languages has also had a powerful impact on the teaching of sign language, an area in which Deaf people have fared reasonably well. Sign language courses began to be offered soon after the publication of the *DASL* in 1965, and both the number of Deaf teachers and their educational levels have increased over the years. In 1982, Battison and Carter reported that 24 percent of sign language teachers were deaf. The percentage had increased to approximately 50 percent by the mid-1990s (Cooper 1997; Blumenthal Kelly 2000). With regard to educational attainment, Battison and Carter reported in 1982 that 84 percent of teachers had a B.A., while Newell in 1995 reported that 50 percent of sign language teachers had an M.A., and 5.8 percent a Ph.D. Cooper (1997) reported 40.3 percent as having an M.A. and 6 percent as having a Ph.D. In addition, as Wilcox (1992) reports, many high schools, colleges, and universities now allow ASL to satisfy foreign language requirements, a development that has sharply increased the need for trained teachers with graduate degrees.

The research that served to legitimize sign languages has helped increase and improve services for Deaf people, such as interpreting. The Registry of Interpreters for the Deaf was established in 1964 and has had a major impact on establishing standards for interpreting between ASL and English, an achievement that would have been impossible without the recognition of ASL as a language. In addition, there is great interest within the interpreting community in research on all aspects of sign language structure, including variation. Interpreters express consistent enthusiasm for workshops and conferences at which research findings are shared, as these findings directly affect the interpreting process. Currently, 175 interpreter training programs operate in the United States, including A.A. and B.A. programs and one M.A. program at Gallaudet University.

Finally, research on sign languages has had an effect on the graduate training of both Deaf and hearing people. The *Linguistics and Language Behavior Abstracts* reports that prior to 1985, Woodward (1973) was the only sign language dissertation. By the 1997–2000 survey period, twenty-seven dissertations had been written at twenty-two universities, including Arizona, Boston, Gallaudet, New Mexico and Rochester.

Thus, the research on sign language structure that William Stokoe initiated and to which Carl Croneberg contributed has ultimately led to a growing understanding of the nature of human language and to the continuing empowerment of Deaf people.

NOTE

1. "Deaf" refers to individuals and groups who regard themselves as culturally Deaf. Lowercased "deaf" refers to audiological status. Glosses of ASL signs are written in small capitals.

REFERENCES

Baker, Charlotte, and Robbin Battison, eds. 1980. *Sign Language and the Deaf Community: Essays in Honor of William C. Stokoe.* Silver Spring, Md.: NAD.

Battison, Robbin, and Mel Carter. 1982. The Academic Acceptance of Sign Language: Teaching American Sign Language as a Second/Foreign Language. In *Proceedings of the Third National Symposium on Sign Language Research and Teaching.* Silver Spring, Md.: NAD.

Battison, Robbin M., Harry Markowicz, and James C. Woodward. 1975. A Good Rule of Thumb: Variable Phonology in American Sign Language. In *Analyzing Variation in Language,* ed. Ralph W. Fasold and Roger Shuy, 291–302. Washington, D.C.: Georgetown University Press.

Blumenthal-Kelly, Arlene. 2000. How deaf women construct teaching, language and culture, and gender and feminism. Doctoral dissertation, University of Maryland, College Park.

Bourgerie, Dana S. 1990. A quantitative study of sociolinguistic variation in Cantonese. Doctoral dissertation, Ohio State University, Columbus.

Cooper, Susan. 1997. The academic status of sign language programs in institutions of higher education in the United States. Doctoral dissertation, Gallaudet University, Washington, D.C.

Emmorey, Karen. 1999. The Confluence of Space and Language in Signed Languages. In *Language and Space,* ed. Paul Bloom et al., 171–209. Cambridge: MIT Press.

Frishberg, Nancy. 1975. Arbitrariness and Iconicity: Historical Change in American Sign Language. *Language* 5(1): 696–719.

Guy, Gregory. 1980. Variation in the Group and the Individual: The Case of Final Stop Deletion. In *Locating Language in Time and Space,* ed. William Labov, 1–36. New York: Academic.

Johnson, Robert E., Scott Liddell, and Carol Erting. 1989. *Unlocking the Curriculum: Principles for Achieving Access in Deaf Education.* Working paper 89-3. Gallaudet Research Institute, Washington, D.C.

Jones, Thomas, and James Achtzehn. 1992. A Century of Leadership. *Gallaudet Today* 22(3): 2–11.

Keep, John. 1857. The Mode of Learning the Sign Language. In *Convention of American Instructors of the Deaf Proceedings,* 133–53.

Labov, William. 1963. The Social Motivation of a Sound Change. *Word* 19: 273–309.

———. 1966. *The Social Stratification of English in New York City.* Washington, D.C.: Center for Applied Linguistics.

Lane, Harlan, Robert Hoffmeister, and Ben Bahan. 1996. *Journey into the DEAF-WORLD.* San Diego: DawnSign.

Liddell, Scott K., and Robert B. Johnson. 1989. American Sign Language: The Phonological Base. *Sign Language Studies* 64: 195–278.

Lucas, Ceil. 1995. Sociolinguistic Variation in ASL: The Case of DEAF. In *Sociolinguistics in Deaf Communities,* vol. 1, ed. Ceil Lucas, 3–25. Washington, D.C.: Gallaudet University Press.

Lucas, Ceil, Robert Bayley, and Clayton Valli. 2001. *Sociolinguistic Variation in American Sign Language.* Washington, D.C.: Gallaudet University Press.

Maher, Jane. 1996. *Seeing Language in Sign: The Work of William C. Stokoe.* Washington, D.C.: Gallaudet University Press.

Newell, William J. 1995. American Sign Language Teachers: Practices and Perceptions. *Sign Language Studies* 87: 141–65.

Shuy, Roger, Walt Wolfram, and William Riley. 1968. *Field Techniques in an Urban Language Study.* Washington, D.C.: Center for Applied Linguistics.

Stokoe, William C. 1994. A Sign Language Dictionary. *The Deaf Way,* ed. Carol Erting et al., 331–34. Washington, D.C.: Gallaudet University Press.

Stokoe, William C., Dorothy Casterline, and Carl Croneberg. 1965. *A Dictionary of American Sign Language on Linguistic Principles.* Silver Spring, Md.: Linstok.

Weinreich, Uriel, William Labov, and Marvin Herzog. 1968. Empirical Foundations for a Theory of Language Change. In *Directions for Historical Linguistics,* ed. Winfred P. Lehmann and Yakov Malkiel, 95–119. Austin: University of Texas Press.

Wilcox, Sherman, ed. 1992. *Academic Acceptance of American Sign Language.* Silver Spring, Md.: Linstok.

Wolfram, Walt. 1969. *A Sociolinguistic Description of Detroit Negro Speech.* Washington, D.C.: Center for Applied Linguistics.

Woodward, James C. 1973. Implicational lects on the Deaf diglossic continuum. Doctoral dissertation, Georgetown University.

Woodward, James C., and Susan DeSantis. 1977. Two to One It Happens: Dynamic Phonology in Two Sign Languages. *Sign Language Studies* 17: 329–46.

Woodward, James C., Carol Erting, and Susanna Oliver. 1976. Facing and Hand(l)ing Variation in American Sign Language. *Sign Language Studies* 10: 43–52.

Lexical Variation in African American and White Signing

Ceil Lucas, Robert Bayley, Ruth Reed, and Alyssa Wulf

This article, part of a larger study of phonological, morphosyntactic, and lexical variation in American Sign Language (ASL), examines lexical differences in the ASL varieties used by African American and white signers. Our goal is to reexamine claims made about the correlation of lexical variation with ethnicity as well as claims pertaining to the course of language change (see, e.g., Woodward 1976). Specifically, we examine three questions: (1) Are there lexical differences between African American and white signing? (2) What are the processes of change reflected in the varieties of ASL used by African American and white signers? (3) How does lexical innovation differ from phonological variation in the lexicon?

To answer these questions, we focus on the responses of ASL signers to picture and fingerspelled stimuli designed to elicit specific lexical items.[1] The elicitation task was part of a much larger study of sociolinguistic variation in ASL, described later in the paper. A brief review of research on lexical variation in ASL and African American signing demonstrates that the same kinds of issues that characterize lexical variation in spoken languages also characterize lexical variation in ASL, for example, phonological variation within the lexicon and occurrences of rapid lexical innovation related to changes in social norms.

PREVIOUS RESEARCH

Lexical Variation

Users and observers of ASL have been aware of variation in the language for a long time, and evidence of this awareness can be seen in writings

This article was originally published in *American Speech* 76(4): 339–60.

about deaf people's language use. For example, Warring Wilkinson (1875), principal of the California School for the Deaf in Berkeley, wrote about how "the sign language" comes about:

> The deaf mute child has mental pictures. He wants to convey similar pictures to his friends. Has speech a genesis in any other fact or need? In the natural order of thought the concrete always precedes the abstract, the subject its attribute, the actor the act. So the deaf mute, like the primitive man, deals primarily with things. He points to an object, and seizing upon some characteristic or dominant feature makes a sign for it. When he has occasion to refer to that object in its absence, he will reproduce the gesture, which will be readily understood, because the symbol has been tacitly agreed upon. Another deaf mute, seeing the same thing, is struck by another peculiarity, and makes another and different sign. Thus half a dozen or more symbols may be devised to represent one and the same thing, and then the principle of the "survival of the fittest" comes in, and the best sign becomes established in usage. (37)

Wilkinson's statement provides some evidence of early awareness of lexical variation, at least among educators of the deaf. However, systematic research did not begin until the 1960s, with Carl Croneberg's two appendices to the *Dictionary of American Sign Language (DASL* 1965). "The Linguistic Community" (Croneberg 1965a) describes the cultural and social aspects of the deaf community and discusses the issues of economic status, patterns of social contact, and the factors that contribute to group cohesion. These factors include the extensive personal and organizational networks that ensure frequent contact even among people who live on opposite sides of the country. "Sign Language Dialects" (Croneberg 1965b) addresses sociolinguistic variation, specifically as it pertains to the preparation of a dictionary:

> One of the problems that early confronts the lexicographers of a language is dialect, and this problem is particularly acute

when the language has never before been written. They must try to determine whether an item in the language is "standard," that is, used by the majority of a given population, or "dialect," that is, used by a particular section of the population. (313)

Croneberg outlines the difference between what he terms *horizontal variation* (regional variation) and *vertical variation* (variation that occurs in the language of groups separated by social stratification) and states that ASL exhibits both. He then describes the results of a study of lexical variation undertaken in North Carolina, Virginia, Maine, New Hampshire, and Vermont using a 134-item sign vocabulary list. He found that for ASL, the state boundaries between North Carolina and Virginia also constitute dialect boundaries. North Carolina signs were not found in Virginia and vice versa. The three New England states were less internally standardized (i.e., people within each state exhibited a wide range of variants for each item), and the state boundaries in New England were much less important, with considerable overlap in lexical choice observed between the three states. Croneberg points out the key role of the residential schools in the dissemination of dialects: "At such a school, the young deaf learn ASL in the particular variety characteristic of the local region. The school is also a source of local innovations, for each school generation comes up with some new signs or modifications of old ones" (314).

In his discussion of vertical variation, Croneberg mentions the influence of age, ethnicity, gender, religion, and status. His definition of status encompasses economic level, occupation, relative leadership within the deaf community, and educational background. He further notes that professionally employed individuals who were financially prosperous graduates of Gallaudet College tend to seek each other out and form a group. Frequently they use certain signs that are considered superior to the signs used locally for the same thing. Examples of such signs are Gallaudet signs, transmitted by one or more graduates of Gallaudet who are now teaching at a school for the deaf and who are members of the local elite. The sign may or may not later be incorporated in the sign language of the local or regional community (318).

Finally, Croneberg comments on what a "standard" sign language might be and states that "few have paid any attention to the term *standard* in the sense of 'statistically most frequent.' The tendency has been to divide sign language into good and bad," with older signers and educators of the deaf maintaining "the superiority of the signs they learned from one or several masters of ASL" (318). He neatly captures the essence of the difference between prescriptive and descriptive perspectives on language when he writes, "What signs the deaf population actually uses and what certain individuals consider good signs are thus very often two completely different things" (319).

A number of studies of lexical variation in ASL were completed in the years following the publication of the *DASL*. Many of the early studies, however, were actually studies of phonological variation, as they almost invariably focused on variation in some parameter of signs, such as handshape (pinky extension, thumb extension), location (on the face, on the hands), or handedness (two-handed or one-handed). For example, in comparing signs that can be produced on the face or on the hands, Woodward, Erting, and Oliver (1976) claim that New Orleans signers in particular and white signers in general produced more signs on the face than signers from Atlanta and African American signers. Woodward and DeSantis (1977), in their study of two-handed signs that can be signed one-handed, claim that African American signers produce more two-handed signs than do white signers, and they describe the variation between two-handed and one-handed signs as "one on-going change" seen in both ASL and French Sign Language. One of the stated goals of their study was "to specify how the change is in the process of occurring" (329) and to demonstrate that the rate of change depends on specific social factors such as age and ethnicity. Frishberg (1975) also examined variation in location and handedness, and Shroyer and Shroyer (1984) presented a broad nontechnical picture of lexical variation in ASL. While many of the variants that they present are actually related phonological variants of the same basic sign, they seem to present them as separate lexical items.

In recent years, the focus of research on lexical variation has broadened considerably. Work undertaken in the last decade includes small-scale studies of various social and occupational categories. Researchers have looked at gender differences (Mansfield 1993), differences in the use of signs for sexual behavior and drug use (Bridges 1993), variation related to socioeconomic status (Shapiro 1993), and lexical variation in the signing produced by interpreters for deaf-blind people (Collins and Petronio 1998).

Research on African American Signing

In his appendices to *DASL*, Croneberg discusses differences between African American and white signing that arose as a consequence of the segregation of deaf schools in the South. Based on responses to the 134-item sign vocabulary list discussed in the previous section, he reports a "radical dialect difference between the signs" of a young North Carolina African American woman and those of white signers living in the same city (1965b, 315). In the following decade, Woodward (1976), in addition to the studies described above, examined African American signing in more detail. He studied three hundred signs produced by African Americans in Georgia and Louisiana and reports that African Americans maintain older forms of signs, while white signers in the same areas have adopted more standard signs.

In recent years, African American signing has been the object of several investigations. Aramburo (1989) and Guggenheim (1993) observed lexical variation during structured but informal interviews. Lewis, Palmer, and Williams (1995) studied the existence of and attitudes toward African American varieties. Specifically, they described the differences in body movement, in mouth movement, and in the use of space in the signing of one African American signer who code-switched during a monologue. In addition, they explored how interpreters handled the code-switching in spoken language from standard English to African American Vernacular English (AAVE). Lewis (1996) continued the examination of African American signing styles in his paper on the parallels between communication styles of hearing and deaf African Americans. His investigation took its departure from two observations: First, ASL users recognize the existence of what is often referred to as "Black signing" but have difficulty in explaining what makes it Black; second, uniquely Black or "ebonic" (Asante 1990) kinesic and nonverbal features exist, and these features occur in the communication of both hearing and deaf African Americans. His investigation described some of these kinesic and nonverbal features—specifically, body postures and rhythmic patterns accompanying the production of signs—in the language used by a deaf adult African American woman. The frequently articulated perspective that African American signing differs markedly from white signing in all areas of structure—including the lexicon—is thus beginning to be explored.

METHODS

To examine variation in ASL, we needed a large videotaped corpus representative of the language as it is used across the United States. The creation of a videotaped corpus immediately raises the question of what is representative of ASL use. The American deaf population is linguistically diverse and comprises numerous Deaf communities (Padden and Humphries 1988).[2] However, as Croneberg (1965b) points out, there is definitely a shared sense of ASL as a language used by Deaf people all across the country. Accompanying this shared sense are shared perceptions that signing varies from region to region, that African American signers sign differently than white signers, and that there exists a "Black ASL" (Aramburo 1989). Many in the American Deaf community also believe that younger signers sign differently than older signers, that men differ from women in their signing, and that as a function of social class working-class Deaf people sign differently than middle-class Deaf professionals. The challenge, then, was to capture on videotape ASL signing that would be representative of the regional, ethnic, age, gender, and socioeconomic diversity within the American Deaf community.

Communities

To obtain a representative sample of regional variation, we selected seven sites: Staunton, Virginia; Frederick, Maryland; Boston, Massachusetts;

Olathe, Kansas; New Orleans, Louisiana; Fremont, California; and Bellingham, Washington. The Olathe site included some signers from Kansas City, Missouri; the Fremont site included some signers from San José; and the Boston site included young signers at the Learning Center for Deaf Children in Framingham, Massachusetts. All of these sites have thriving communities of ASL users. In addition, Staunton, Frederick, Boston, Fremont, and Olathe have residential schools for deaf children, all with long-established surrounding Deaf communities. A basic motivation in the selection of the sites was to represent major areas of the country—Northeast, East, South, Midwest, West, and Northwest. Since they are within driving distance of Washington, D.C., the sites of Gallaudet University, where the larger project was based, Staunton, and Frederick served as the pilot sites. In the late summer and early fall of 1994, we tested and refined the data collection methodology before implementing it in the other five sites. Data were collected in Boston in January 1995, in Olathe/Kansas City in May 1995, in Fremont and Bellingham in June 1995, and in New Orleans in September 1995. The overall organization of the larger project is shown in the appendix.

Participants

Deaf people in the United States have many different backgrounds and learn to sign at various times in their lives. Since our focus is on variation in ASL rather than on acquisition, we set out to recruit native or near-native ASL users, including Deaf individuals from Deaf families who learned to sign natively in the home as well as Deaf individuals who learned to sign before age 5 or 6 from their peers in residential schools. To control for the effects of late- and second-language acquisition as much as possible, we did not recruit individuals who, while competent adult users of ASL, learned to sign as adolescents either because they lacked exposure to the language or were born hearing and were native speakers of English before losing their hearing.

The sample included both white and African American signers in four sites, Boston, New Orleans, Olathe/Kansas City, and Fremont, where a sufficient number of African American Deaf people live to make data collection possible. The goal was to gather empirical evidence of the differences that signers feel exist between the signing of African Americans and that of whites.

Participants were recruited in three different age groups: 15–25, 26–54, and 55+. The division of participants into age groups was motivated by developments in language policy in deaf education. Specifically, the early 1970s witnessed both the passage of Public Law 94-142 (the Education of All Handicapped Children Act of 1975, resulting in the implementation of mainstreaming policies) and the shift from purely oral methods of instruction to the philosophy of Total Communication (Ramsey 1989; Nover 1995).[3] The consequence for the acquisition of ASL is that children who previously might have been sent to residential schools and exposed to ASL by their peers (when oral methods dominated in the classroom) may now be mainstreamed with hearing children and not be exposed to ASL until much later, if at all.

Children in residential schools, while still using ASL among themselves, now are often exposed to Total Communication in the classroom. At the same time, ASL has been implemented as the medium of instruction in several locations since the mid-1980s, including two of our sites (Fremont and Boston), and the recognition of ASL as a full-fledged language independent from English has increased dramatically in recent years.

Participants in the 15–25 age group could be expected to have been exposed to Total Communication (and possibly to ASL) as the medium of instruction and to increased awareness of the status of ASL. Participants in the 26–54 group would have been exposed to oralism and would also have witnessed the change to Total Communication and the beginning of changes in attitudes about ASL resulting from Stokoe's pioneering work in the early 1960s. Finally, participants in the 55+ group would most likely have been educated in residential schools through the oral method and possibly also through fingerspelling, with ASL tolerated in the dormitories but certainly not in the classroom. In fact, some participants in the oldest group told the familiar story of being physically punished for using ASL in class.

Our sample also included both working-class and middle-class women and men. Although social class has long been a major focus of sociolinguistic research on spoken languages, the relationship between linguistic variation and socioeconomic status has not previously been examined closely in ASL. To define social classes, we followed demographic studies of the deaf community (Schein and Delk 1974; Schein 1987). Working-class participants had not continued their education past high school (in some cases, not past elementary school or eighth grade) and worked in blue-collar occupations. In most cases, they had also lived their entire lives in the places where they grew up and went to school. By contrast, middle-class participants had completed college (and in many cases earned graduate degrees), were working in professional positions, and often had left their home areas to go to school but had since returned and settled. In all seven sites, we were able to recruit participants in every age group and socioeconomic level except middle-class African Americans in the 55+ age group. This is striking and sad evidence of the double discrimination confronting deaf African Americans of this generation.

Data Collection

The approach to participants was informed by the work of Labov (1984) and Milroy (1987). Groups of three to seven individuals were assembled in each area by a contact person, a Deaf individual who lived in the area, knew the local community well, and was a respected member of it. These contact persons were similar to the "brokers" described by Milroy, people who "have contacts with large numbers of individuals" in the community (10). In some cases, the contact persons also participated in data collection sessions. Sessions took place in three phases. The first phase consisted of approximately one hour of free conversation among participants without the researchers present. In the second phase, two participants were selected from each group and interviewed in depth by the Deaf researchers about their backgrounds, their social networks, and their patterns of language use. The last phase, and the focus of this article, involved an elicitation task. All of the participants being interviewed were shown the same set of thirty-four stimuli (pictures and fingerspelled words) and asked to supply signs for the objects or actions represented. All three phases were videotaped.

Analysis

The analysis presented here is based on the responses of 140 of the 207 participants in the four research sites where we were able to elicit data from both African American and white signers: Boston, New Orleans, Olathe/Kansas City, and Fremont. Table 1 summarizes the demographic characteristics of the participants focused on here.

The thirty-four stimuli are as follows: AFRICA, ARREST, BANANA, CAKE, CANDY, CEREAL, CHEAT, CHERRIES, CHICKEN, COMPUTER, DEER, DELICIOUS, DOG, EARLY, FAINT, FEAR, GLOVES, JAPAN, MICROWAVE, MITTENS, PANTS (men's), PANTS (women's), PERFUME, PIZZA, RABBIT, RELAY, RUN, SANDWICH, SNOW, SOON, SQUIRREL, STEAL, THIEF, and TOMATO.

These stimuli were chosen on the basis of earlier work on lexical variation. All are signs for which we expected to see considerable variation. For some signs, based on the work of Woodward, Erting, and Oliver (1976) and Woodward and DeSantis (1977), we expected to see phonological processes such as assimilation, deletion, and neutralization at work (e.g., the handshapes in a two-handed sign such as TOMATO changing to match each other; the first sign in a sign such as SNOW [WHITE⌒FALL] being deleted; or signs produced at the forehead, such as RABBIT, being lowered to be produced in the space in front of the signer). Furthermore, Shroyer and Shroyer (1984) show considerable variation in specific semantic categories, such as food and animals, so we included signs in these categories. Finally, a number of new signs have been introduced over the last fifteen years for reasons of cultural sensitivity, and we wanted to compare these new signs to older signs for the same concepts.

FINDINGS

For 28 of the 34 signs sampled, African Americans used signs that none of the white signers used. The only 6 signs for which the African American

Table 1. Signer Social and Demographic Characteristics

	Boston	New Orleans	Olathe/ Kansas City	Fremont	Total
Age					
15–25	9	7	12	6	34
26–54	12	15	16	16	59
55+	9	12	14	12	47
Social Class					
Working	17	20	26	18	81
Middle	13	14	16	16	59
Gender					
Male	15	17	20	16	68
Female	15	17	22	18	72
Ethnicity					
African American	11	13	14	15	53
White	19	21	28	19	87
Language Background					
ASL	5	8	7	11	31
Other	25	26	35	23	109
Total	30	34	42	34	140

signers did not have unique variants were CAKE, MICROWAVE, JAPAN, SAND-
WICH, THIEF, and STEAL. In this paper, we focus on the results for RABBIT,
DEER, TOMATO, SNOW, JAPAN, and AFRICA. JAPAN and AFRICA both have
fairly new variants that coexist with indigenous ASL signs, the new variants having been introduced for reasons of cultural sensitivity. RABBIT,
DEER, TOMATO, and SNOW provide insight into ongoing phonological
variation and possible change. RABBIT can be produced at the forehead
or in the space in front of the signer; DEER can be produced with one or
two hands; TOMATO can be produced with two different handshapes (a
1 handshape for the active hand and a flat O or an S for the base hand)
or with identical handshapes, the result of assimilation; SNOW can be produced as a compound, WHITE⌢SUBSTANCE-FALL, or simply as SUBSTANCE-
FALL. Figures 1–4 illustrate the key variants for RABBIT, DEER, SNOW, and
TOMATO.

Tables 2–5 show the breakdown of variants for each of these four
signs by ethnicity. In each table, we have noted the number of separate
lexical items produced for the stimulus and the main features of those
signs. The +/− simply indicates whether the sign in question was used or
not by African American and white signers; + and − do not have numer-
ical values.

Each number in the tables represents a separate lexical item. For
example, the stimulus RABBIT elicited three lexical items, and TOMATO
elicited five. In many cases, these items (or signs) exhibit phonological
variation. In the case of RABBIT in Table 2, the two variants of the first lexical item are produced with the H handshape (variants 1a and 1b). The
first variant, the low form, is produced in neutral space. The second variant is produced with the same handshape at the level of the head.
However, a separate sign, a bent V handshape, is produced on the forehead with the palm out (variant 3). This form is a separate lexical item
and not a phonological variant of the lexical item meaning RABBIT that is
produced with an H handshape (variant 1). The situation is analogous to
lexical variation in spoken languages. In American English, for example,
"couch," "sofa," and "davenport" are separate lexical items that refer to the

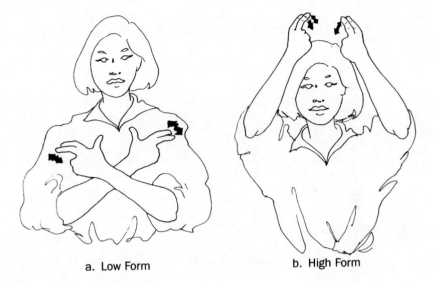

a. Low Form   b. High Form

Figure 1.

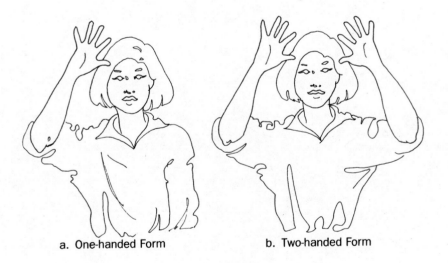

a. One-handed Form   b. Two-handed Form

Figure 2.

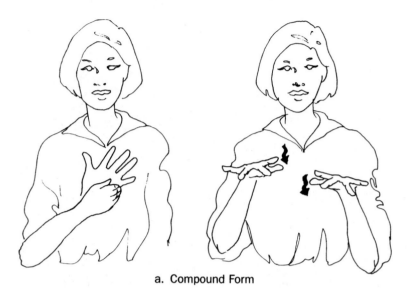

a. Compound Form

b. Noncompound Form

Figure 3.

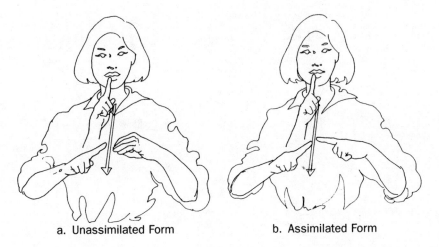

a. Unassimilated Form   b. Assimilated Form

Figure 4.

same piece of furniture. Like any other lexical items, they are also subject to processes of phonological variation and change and may exhibit regional and social differences in pronunciation. In the case of RABBIT, a lexicalized fingerspelled variant is indicated by #. Signers may choose to represent a lexical item by using the manual alphabet illustrated in Figure 5.

Table 2. Signs for RABBIT

Sign	White	African American	Description
1a	+	+	Low form, in neutral space, H handshape
1b	+	+	Some variant of head form, H handshape
2	–	+	Fingerspell #RABBIT
3	–	+	Bent V handshape on forehead, palm out, wiggle

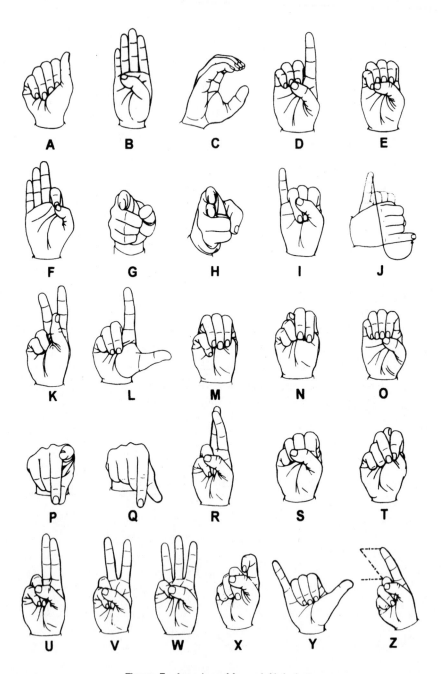

Figure 5. American Manual Alphabet

Table 3. Signs for DEER

Sign	White	African American	Description
1a	+	+	One-handed or two-handed 5 handshape on temple, move up and away
1b	+	+	Two-handed 5 handshape on temple
1c	+	+	One-handed 5 handshape on side of temple
1d	–	+	Two-handed Y handshape or 5 handshape on forehead
2	–	+	Fingerspell #DEER
3	+	+	Two-handed bent 3 handshape on temple
4	+	–	One-handed I-LOVE-YOU handshape on forehead

Table 4. Signs for SNOW

Sign	White	African American	Description
1a	+	+	Compound WHITE + 5 handshape wiggle
1b	+	+	5 handshape wiggle only (no WHITE)
1c	–	+	Same as FREEZE
1d	+	–	F handshape at shoulder, palm in, then 5 handshape wiggle
2	–	+	Fingerspell #SNOW, then 5 handshape wiggle

Table 5. Signs for TOMATO

Sign	White	African American	Description
1a	+	+	Nondominant hand is flat O, baby O, S or open S (non-assimilated)
1b	+	+	Both hands are index or H (assimilated)
2	–	+	Two-handed 5 handshape, dominant hand crosses back of base hand
3	+	+	Fingerspell #TOMATO
4	+	+	Classifier: BALL or RED; classifier: BALL
5	–	+	T handshape on cheek, twist

Sometimes each letter is represented clearly and separately. This is indicated with dashes, as in A-F-R-I-C-A in Table 7 on the next page. However, as the result of widespread use and repetition, a sequence of fingerspelled letters may begin to look like a sign, that is, it becomes lexicalized. This is the case in #RABBIT.

Table 6. Signs for JAPAN

Sign	White	African American	Description
1a	+	+	Variant of "new" sign (outline of Japanese islands)
2	+	+	Variant of J or 1 handshape at the eye

Table 7. Signs for AFRICA

Sign	White	African American	Description
1	+	+	New sign: outline continent
2	+	+	A or 8 handshape, circle face, may end on nose
3	−	+	A handshape, thumb brushes forehead like BLACK
4	−	+	F handshape, ring in nose
5	−	+	Fingerspell #AFRICA

RABBIT, as seen in Table 2, is produced both by African American and white signers at the forehead location and in the neutral space location, but only African American signers fingerspelled #RABBIT and produced a form on the forehead with a bent V handshape, palm out. Table 3 shows that both African American and white signers produce the one-handed and the two-handed variants of DEER, while only the African American signers fingerspelled #DEER and only the white signers produced a variant on the forehead with the so-called I-LOVE-YOU handshape, with thumb, index, and pinky extended. Table 4 shows that African American and white signers use both the compound and reduced forms of SNOW, but only the African American signers produce a combined form of fingerspelling and signing (variant 2). Both African American and white signers produce nonassimilated and assimilated forms of TOMATO, as seen in Table 5, as well as fingerspelled forms and forms iconic of a round shape. Only the African American signers produced a T handshape twisting on the cheek and a 5 handshape across the back of the base hand for TOMATO.

Figures 6 and 7 illustrate the key variants for JAPAN and AFRICA. Table 6 shows that both African American and white signers use both forms of JAPAN: the older form of a J at the side of the eye and the newer form, which is an iconic representation of the islands of Japan. Table 7 shows

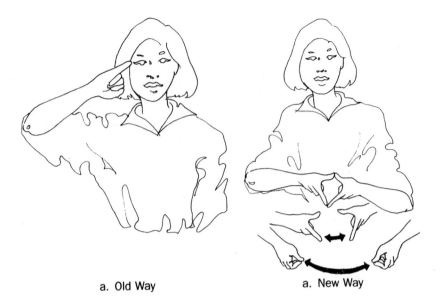

a. Old Way   a. New Way

Figure 6.

a. Old Way   a. New Way

Figure 7.

the distribution of the five variants for AFRICA found in the data. Both African American and white signers use the form that circles the face, the form that outlines the continent, and a fingerspelled form of the sign. Only African American signers in Boston produced variants 3 and 4.

DISCUSSION

This discussion responds to the three questions raised in the introduction. First, there clearly are lexical differences between African American and white signing. For 28 of the 34 stimuli, the African American signers used signs that the white signers did not, including variants of five of the six signs focused on here. While African American and white signers share a lexicon to a great extent, not all areas of the lexicon overlap.

Second, both African American and white signers participate in phonological variation in the lexicon. The key question here is whether this variation is evidence of ongoing or completed change. Recall that earlier studies claimed that white signers produced more signs such as RABBIT on the face than did African American signers (Woodward, Erting, and Oliver 1976) and that African American signers produced more two-handed variants of signs like DEER than did white signers (Woodward and DeSantis 1977). In the data upon which the present study is based, collected more than twenty years after the studies of Woodward and his colleagues, both African American and white signers still produce both the forehead and neutral space forms of RABBIT and the two-handed and one-handed variants of DEER. Neither group uses the one-handed or two-handed form exclusively. If we are seeing change in progress, it is not completed. If the claims of the earlier research were borne out, we might expect to see only African American signers using the hand version of RABBIT and all signers using only one-handed DEER. Of course, we may simply be witnessing stable variation. The same holds true for the nonassimilated and assimilated forms of TOMATO and the compound and noncompound forms of SNOW. Both the African American and the white signers in the sample used nonassimilated and assimilated forms of TOMATO and the compound and noncompound forms of SNOW. If change were completed for either group, we might expect to see only assimilated and noncompound variants of these signs. And when we look at the use of these different variants across the three age groups in the study (15–25, 26–54, 55+), we see that signers in all three age groups use all variants (age-group results reported in Lucas, Bayley, and Valli 2001). That is, there is no variant exclusive to one age group.

Third, we see a clear need to distinguish phonological variation in the lexicon from lexical innovation. RABBIT, DEER, SNOW, and TOMATO provide examples of predictable phonological variation and change within the lexicon, as seen in the variable location in RABBIT, variable handedness in DEER, the possible deletion of a syllable in SNOW, and handshape assimilation in TOMATO (also technically a compound, formed from the signs RED and SLICE). All four signs are indigenous to ASL, and the phonological processes that apply to them are at work elsewhere in the language.

However, the new forms for AFRICA and JAPAN entered the language in a very different way. These signs are examples of fairly rapid lexical innovation, both cases in which new forms were introduced to respond to specific societal or political pressures. The new form of JAPAN is the sign used in Japanese Sign Language to name the country. It was borrowed into ASL in the late 1980s at the same time that many other country signs were being borrowed and were beginning to replace indigenous ASL signs. This borrowing was the direct result of the increased contact between American Deaf people and Deaf people from communities all over the world. One well-known occasion for intense contact was the Deaf Way conference and arts festival held at Gallaudet University in Washington, D.C., in 1989, with more than six thousand people in attendance from the Americas, Europe, Asia, and Africa. Common reasons cited for the borrowing are to show respect for other cultures and to avoid imposing the ASL sign on the Deaf citizens of other nations, who have signs in their own languages for their respective countries. Also, the indigenous ASL signs for CHINA, KOREA, and JAPAN, which iconically refer to perceived Asian eye shapes, are often seen as racist. The acceptance of other signing traditions is no doubt in part a reflection of the anger that

American Deaf people have felt at having their own language tampered with by educators and educational administrators.

The new sign for AFRICA, on the other hand, is believed to have been introduced as a direct response to older ASL signs for AFRICA that focus on the nose and are also widely believed to be racist. This is not a sign which originated in AFRICA; rather, deaf folklore has it that the sign was proposed by one person during a formal lecture, although there are various accounts of this event. Ironically, notwithstanding its widespread use by the signers in our sample, recent anecdotal evidence suggests that both African and African American signers are expressing a preference for the A handshape variant that simply circles the face (with no contact on the nose) and are rejecting the new sign in part because it closely resembles the sign for a part of the female anatomy (Aramburo, personal communication, 1989).

Furthermore, AFRICA and JAPAN do show some differences among the age groups in the study. Specifically, African American signers in the 55+ group in Kansas and white signers in the 55+ group in Virginia do not use the new sign for JAPAN at all, while signers in the 15–25 group in Virginia and Maryland do not use the old sign at all. Signers in the 55+ age group in Louisiana and Kansas, both African American and white, do not use the new sign for AFRICA, while signers in the 15–25 group in California (both African American and white), Virginia, and Maryland do not use the A-on-the-face variant at all. So, unlike the signs that show phonological variation and change (RABBIT, DEER, TOMATO, SNOW), the lexical innovation represented by JAPAN and AFRICA is not found across all age groups and may even be resisted by signers in the older age groups.

CONCLUSION

The results presented here show that lexical differences between African American and white signing persist, but the claims of earlier research are not completely borne out. Also, just as in studies of lexical variation in spoken language, studies of variation in sign language need to distinguish between phonological variation and change and rapid lexical innovation and diffusion. Finally, more detailed quantitative analysis of the distribution of the variants examined here and elsewhere is needed to explore more fully the possible direction of change and differences among various social and regional groups.

APPENDIX

Project on Sociolinguistic Variation in ASL

Data Collection

1. Staunton, Virginia	5. Fremont, California
2. Frederick, Maryland	6. Olathe, Kansas/Kansas City, Missouri
3. Boston, Massachusetts	7. Bellingham, Washington
4. New Orleans, Louisiana	

Twelve groups at each site, except for Staunton, Frederick, and Bellingham (only white groups):

African American		White	
Middle Class	Working Class	Middle Class	Working Class
15–25	15–25	15–25	15–25
26–54	26–54	26–54	26–54
—*	55+	55+	55+

*It was not possible to locate African American participants in the 55+ age group. Owing to the burdens of double discrimination, very few deaf African Americans in this age group managed to reach middle-class status.

A total of 207 ASL signers, with each group consisting of 2–7 signers.

OVERALL GOAL OF THE PROJECT

A description of phonological, morphosyntactic, and lexical variation in ASL and the correlation of variation with external factors such as age, gender, ethnicity, and socioeconomic status.

Phonological: the sign DEAF, the location of signs represented by the verb KNOW, signs made with a 1 handshape
Morphosyntactic: overt and null subject pronouns
Lexical: Thirty-four signs selected to illustrate phonological change as well as lexical innovation stemming from new technology, increased contact with Deaf people in other countries, and contemporary social attitudes.

We gratefully acknowledge Gallaudet University Press for the use of the manual alphabet chart, Robert Walker for the illustrations, and MJ Bienvenu and Erin Wilkinson as the sign models.

REFERENCES

Aramburo, Anthony. 1989. Sociolinguistic Aspects of the Black Deaf Community. In *The Sociolinguistics of the Deaf Community*, ed. Ceil Lucas, 103–19. San Diego: Academic.

Asante, Molefi K. 1990. African Elements in African American English. In *Africanisms in American Culture*, ed. Joseph E. Holloway, 19–23. Bloomington: Indiana University Press.

Bridges, Byron. 1993. Gender variation with sex signs. Department of ASL, Linguistics, and Interpretation, Gallaudet University unpublished ms.

Collins, Steven, and Karen Petronio. 1998. What Happens in Tactile ASL? In *Pinky Extension and Eye Gaze: Language Use in Deaf communities*, ed. Ceil Lucas, 18–37. Washington, D.C.: Gallaudet University Press.

Croneberg, Carl. 1965a. The Linguistic Community. Appendix C in *DASL*, 297–311.

———. 1965b. Sign Language Dialects. Appendix D in *DASL*, 313–19.

Denton, David M. 1976. *The Philosophy of Total Communication: Supplement to the British Deaf News, August 1976*. Carlisle, England: British Deaf Association.

Frishberg, Nancy. 1975. Arbitrariness and Iconicity: Historical Change in American Sign Language. *Language* 51: 696–719.

Guggenheim, Laurie. 1993. Ethnic Variation in ASL: The Signing of African Americans and How It Is Influenced by Conversational Topic. In *Communication Forum*, ed. Elizabeth Winston, 51–76. Washington, D.C.: Department of ASL, Linguistics, and Interpretation, Gallaudet University.

Johnson, Robert E., Scott K. Liddell, and Carol J. Erting. 1989. *Unlocking the Curriculum: Principles for Achieving Access in Deaf Education*. Gallaudet Research Institute Working Paper 89-3. Washington, D.C.: Gallaudet University.

Labov, William. 1984. Field Methods of the Project on Language Change and Variation. In *Language in Use: Readings in Sociolinguistics*, ed. John Baugh and Joel Sherzer, 28–53. Englewood Cliffs, N.J.: Prentice-Hall.

Lewis, John. 1996. Parallels in Communication Styles of Hearing and Deaf African Americans. Gallaudet University unpublished ms.

Lewis, John, Carrie Palmer, and Leandra Williams. 1995. Existence of and Attitudes toward Black Variations of Sign Language. In *Communication Forum*, ed. Laura Byers, Jessica Chaiken, and Monica Mueller, 17–48. Washington, D.C.: Department of ASL, Linguistics, and Interpretation, Gallaudet University.

Lucas, Ceil, Robert Bayley, and Clayton Valli. 2001. *Sociolinguistic Variation in American Sign Language*. Sociolinguistics in Deaf Communities, vol. 7. Washington, D.C.: Gallaudet University Press.

Mansfield, Doris. 1993. Gender Differences in ASL: A Sociolinguistic Study of Sign Choices by Deaf Native Signers. In *Communication Forum*, ed. Elizabeth Winston, 86–98. Washington, D.C.: Department of ASL, Linguistics, and Interpretation, Gallaudet University.

Milroy, Lesley. 1987. *Observing and Analyzing Natural Language*. Oxford: Blackwell.

Nover, Stephen M. 1995. American Sign Language and English in Deaf Education. In *Sociolinguistics in Deaf Communities*, ed. Ceil Lucas, 109–63. Sociolinguistics in Deaf Communities, vol. 1. Washington, D.C.: Gallaudet University Press.

Padden, Carol, and Tom Humphries. 1988. *Deaf in America: Voices from a Culture.* Cambridge: Harvard University Press.

Ramsey, Claire L. 1989. Language Planning in Deaf Education. In *The Sociolinguistics of the Deaf Community,* ed. Ceil Lucas, 123–26. San Diego: Academic.

Schein, Jerome D. 1987. The Demography of Deafness. In *Understanding Deafness Socially,* ed. Paul Higgins and Jeffrey Nash, 3–28. Springfield, Ill.: Thomas.

Schein, Jerome D., and Marcus T. Delk. 1974. *The Deaf Population of the United States.* Silver Spring, Md.: National Association of the Deaf.

Shapiro, Eric. 1993. Socioeconomic Variation in American Sign Language. In *Communication Forum,* ed. Elizabeth Winston, 150–75. Washington, D.C.: Department of ASL, Linguistics, and Interpretation, Gallaudet University.

Shroyer, Edgar, and Susan Shroyer. 1984. *Signs across America: A Look at Regional Differences in American Sign Language.* Washington, D.C.: Gallaudet College Press.

Stokoe, William C. 1960. *Sign Language Structure: An Outline of the Visual Communication System of the American Deaf.* Occasional Papers 8. Buffalo, N.Y.: Department of Linguistics, University of Buffalo.

Stokoe Jr., William C., Dorothy C. Casterline, and Carl G. Croneberg. 1965. *Dictionary of American Sign Language on Linguistic Principles, A (DASL).* Washington, D.C.: Gallaudet Press.

Wilkinson, Warring. 1875. *Eleventh Report of the Board of Directors and Officers of the California Institution for the Education of the Deaf and Blind.* Sacramento.

Woodward, James C. 1976. Black Southern Signing. *Language in Society* 5: 211–18.

Woodward, James C., and Susan DeSantis. 1977. Two to One It Happens: Dynamic Phonology in Two Sign Languages. *Sign Language Studies* 17: 329–46.

Woodward, James C., Carol J. Erting, and Susanna Oliver. 1976. Facing and Hand(l)ing Variation in American Sign Language. *Sign Language Studies* 10: 43–52.

NOTES

1. Fingerspelling is the representation of written words by means of the manual alphabet (see Figure 5). For some signs, such as CHEAT and DELICIOUS, a suitable picture could not be found, and the participants responded to the fingerspelled words for these concepts. (By convention, English glosses of ASL signs are written in small capital letters.)

2. Capitalized "Deaf" designates a cultural affiliation with the Deaf community and ASL; lower-case "deaf" indicates audiological status. Individuals who are deaf may not be Deaf.

3. Oralism is the practice in deaf education of using spoken language as the medium of instruction, to the exclusion of sign language. This practice dominated in deaf education from 1880 until the early 1970s, when the philosophy of Total Communication was introduced (Denton 1976). This philosophy in practice stresses the simultaneous use of speaking and signing. This sign-supported speech (Johnson, Liddell, and Erting 1989) is completely different structurally from natural sign languages such as ASL.

Sociolinguistic Variation

Ceil Lucas, Robert Bayley, Clayton Valli, Mary Rose
and Alyssa Wulf

[George Trager and Henry Lee Smith] insisted that language could not be studied by itself, in isolation, but must be looked at in direct connection to the people who used it, the things they used it to talk about, and the view of the world that using it imposed on them.

STOKOE (1994, 333)

Language varies both in space and in time, as well as according to the linguistic environment in which a form is used. For example, the American Sign Language (ASL) sign DEAF[1] has three possible forms. It can be produced with a movement from ear to chin (the citation or dictionary form), with a movement from chin to ear, or simply by contacting the cheek once (both noncitation forms). Even though the form of DEAF varies from signer to signer and even within the signing of the same signer, the variation we observe is far from random. Rather, signers' choices among the three forms of DEAF are systematically constrained by a range of factors at both the linguistic and the social levels. Thus, compared to signers in other parts of the USA, signers in Boston, Massachusetts, tend to be quite conservative in the choice of a form of DEAF. In contrast, signers in Kansas, Missouri, and Virginia tend to prefer noncitation forms. Indeed, a recent study conducted by three of the authors of this chapter showed that signers in these states used noncitation forms of DEAF 85 percent of the time,

Source. Reprinted by permission of the publisher from C. Lucas, ed., *The Sociolinguistics of Sign Languages* (2001): 61–111. Cambridge: Cambridge University Press. Copyright © 2001 by Cambridge University Press. The references for this reading can be found in the original volume.

111

more than twice the rate of signers in Boston (Bayley et al. 2000; Lucas et al. 2001).

The region of the country where a signer lives is not the only factor that affects the choice of a form of DEAF. For example, although ASL signers in Boston generally used more citation forms of DEAF than signers in other areas of the USA, Boston signers aged 55 and over were far less likely to choose a noncitation form of DEAF than were younger signers. Bayley et al. (2000) reported that Boston signers aged 55 and over used the citation form of DEAF 76 percent of the time. In contrast, signers aged between 26 and 54 used the citation form only 54 percent of the time, and signers aged between 15 and 25 used the citation form only 46 percent of the time. In addition, variation can be affected by linguistic factors. To continue with the example of DEAF, Lucas (1995) and Bayley et al. (2000) found that signers were very likely to use a noncitation form of DEAF when it was part of a compound, as in DEAF⁀CULTURE or DEAF⁀WORLD. However, when DEAF was a predicate adjective, as in PRO.1 DEAF ("I am deaf"), signers were likely to choose the citation form.

As the example of variation in the form of DEAF shows, choices among variable linguistic forms are affected both by social (e.g., region, age) and by linguistic (e.g., grammatical class) factors or constraints. In this chapter, we review the study of language variation, with particular emphasis on the insights that such study can provide into language structure and social relations. We pay special attention to the many intersecting social factors that can influence variation and to the kinds of linguistic units and processes that vary in sign and spoken languages. We conclude with a detailed examination of three studies that represent some of the different types of research on variation in sign languages.

THE STUDY OF LINGUISTIC VARIATION

We begin our discussion of linguistic variation by examining the concept of the "sociolinguistic variable." This leads to an examination of the kinds of units that can be variable in spoken languages and the processes that govern variation. Although our interest in this chapter is primarily sign languages, research on spoken language has provided much of the framework within which research on variation in sign languages has been conducted.

The Sociolinguistic Variable

Several researchers have offered useful explanations of the concept of a *sociolinguistic variable*. Drawing upon the work of Labov (1972a, 1972b), Fasold characterized the sociolinguistic variable as "a set of alternative ways of saying the same thing, although the alternatives will have social significance" (1990, 223–24). Lesley Milroy referred to the "bits of language" that "are associated with sex, area and age subgroups in an extremely complicated way" (1987b, 131), the "bits of language" being sociolinguistic variables. She defined a sociolinguistic variable as "a linguistic element (phonological usually, in practice) which co-varies not only with other linguistic elements, but also with a number of extralinguistic independent social variables such as social class, age, sex, ethnic group or contextual style" (1987b, 10). Wolfram defined a linguistic variable as a "convenient construct employed to unite a class of fluctuating variants within some specified language set" (1991, 23). He drew the distinction between a linguistic variable, which has to do with variation within a language, and a sociolinguistic variable, a construct that unifies the correlation of internal variables and external constraints. Internal variables are the features of a linguistic nature—a sound, a handshape, a syntactic structure—that vary. External constraints are the factors of a social nature that may correlate with the behavior of the linguistic variable.

Variable Units in Spoken Languages

Linguists generally accept that spoken languages are composed of segments of sound produced by the vocal apparatus and that these segments are themselves composed of a variety of features. In spoken languages, whole segments or features of segments may be variable. For example, a word-final voiced consonant may be devoiced, a nonnasal vowel may acquire the feature of nasalization, and vowels may vary from their canonical position and be raised or lowered within the vowel space.

A new segment may also be created from the features of other segments, as often happens in palatalization. Individual segments may be variably added or deleted, and syllables (that is, groups of segments) can be added or deleted. Parts of segments, whole segments, or groups of segments can also be variably rearranged, as we see with metathesis in English, in the variable pronunciations "hundred" and "hunderd."

Variation may also be seen in word-sized combinations of segments or in combinations of words. In lexical variation, we find separate morphemes for the same concept, and use of these separate morphemes correlates with nonlinguistic categories such as region, ethnicity and gender. But we may also see syntactic variation characterized by the deletion of whole morphemes or by the variable position of whole morphemes. Variation is also present in units of discourse (i.e., units consisting of many words), as in variation in text type or in lists used in narratives (Schiffrin 1994). What varies in spoken languages, then, may range from the features of a segment to a discourse unit that consists of many segments, from the very smallest unit we can identify to the largest.

It is evident even to a casual observer that people vary in their use of linguistic forms. At the level of phonology, speakers of English sometimes pronounce the progressive morpheme -ing with the apical variant /n/ (as in workin') and sometimes with the velar nasal /ŋ/ (Fischer 1958; Trudgill 1974; Houston 1991). Speakers of all dialects of English also sometimes delete the final /t/ in words such as *mist* in *mist by the lake* and sometimes pronounce it *mis,* as in *mis/t/ my bus* (Shuy et al. 1968; Labov et al. 1968; Guy 1980; Labov 1997; Roberts 1997). It is important to note here that what is being deleted may be a morpheme, i.e., a segment with independent meaning, as in *mis/t/.* Numerous studies have shown that language varies at the level of morphology. For example, speakers of many English dialects variably use third-person singular verbal -s, as in *he want/he wants* (Poplack and Tagliamonte 1989; Godfrey and Tagliamonte 1999), while learners of English as a second language exhibit great variability in the extent to which they mark past-reference verbs for tense (Bayley 1994b).

Language also varies at the level of syntax. Speakers of Spanish and many other languages as well as ASL signers, for example, sometimes use an overt subject pronoun and sometimes omit it (Poplack 1979; Cameron 1993; Wulf et al. 1999), as shown in (1), from Spanish, and (2), from ASL:

1. Yo/Ø quiero ir a la playa.
   "I want to go to the beach."
2. PRO.1/Ø WANT MEET PRO.3
   "I want to meet him/her."

In addition, in English, the alternation between pied-piped relative pronouns and stranded prepositions provides a convenient example of syntactic variation (Guy and Bayley 1995), for example:

3a. To whom did you give the money?
3b. Who(m) did you give the money to?

Furthermore, as Poplack (1980), Lucas and Valli (1992), Zentella (1997), and others have shown, language users vary in their choice of code. Thus, ASL signers sometimes alternate between ASL and Signed English, and many bilingual speakers alternate between two (or more) languages in the same discourse and often even within the same sentence; for example:

4a. *La* security *viene pa' chequear el* building.
   "Security comes to check the building."
4b. PRO.1 NOT SAY-ING 100 PERCENT SUPPORT, NO . . .
   "I'm not saying 100% support, no . . ." (with a sign produced for the suffix -*ing* and continuous English mouthing).

Variable Processes in Spoken Languages

These examples lead us to ask what kinds of processes are involved in spoken language variation. Our discussion here takes its departure from

Wolfram's (1991, 1993) work on variation in spoken languages. One set of processes involved in variation has to do with the phonological component of a language. For example, variation may be the result of the process of assimilation, such as vowel nasalization or consonant gemination. Variation may result from weakening, as in vowel or consonant deletion. We may see variation resulting from the processes of substitution or addition of elements, as with coalescence (the creation of a new segment from two other segments), metathesis (the rearranging of the order of segments or features of segments) or epenthesis (the addition of a segment). Variation may result from analogy, as in the generalization of third-person singular -s to other present-tense forms of a verb in English or, conversely, the deletion of third-person singular -s by analogy with all other verb forms in a given paradigm.

As we see from the examples, other processes involved with variation may have to do with the morphosyntactic structure of a language. For example, variation may have to do with the process of the co-occurrence of items in syntactic structure. We examine negative concord in English more closely below, whereby some varieties allow the co-occurrence of more than one negative element while other varieties disallow such co-occurrence. Another process involved in variation at the syntactic level concerns permutation of items within sentences. The variable placement of adverbs in English provides a convenient example:

5a. *Quickly,* John ran to the door.
5b. John *quickly* ran to the door.
5c. John ran *quickly* to the door.
5d. John ran to the door *quickly.*

Internal Constraints

This brings us to what the internal constraints on variation might be in spoken languages. Recall that internal constraints on variation are features within the immediate linguistic environment that may play some role in the occurrence of variation. Wolfram (personal communication, 1994) has stated that the internal constraints on variables may be compositional, sequential, functional, or having to do with structural incorporation. Compositional constraints are those that have to do with the linguistic nature of the variable itself. For example, Wolfram (1989) studied final nasal absence in the speech of three-year-old African American children. He found that final alveolar nasals were much more likely to be absent than either velar or bilabial nasals. A sequential constraint has to do with the role of an element occurring in the same sequence as the variable, either preceding or following it. For example, the final consonant in a word-final consonant cluster is more likely to be deleted if the following segment is another consonant than if it is a vowel. Functional constraints relate to the function of the variable. For example, as explained above, the final consonant in a word-final consonant cluster may function as a past-tense morpheme, and that function may influence the frequency of deletion of this consonant. Finally, the constraint of structural incorporation concerns the syntactic environment in which a variable finds itself. For example, copula deletion in African American Vernacular English (AAVE) is more likely in a construction with *gonna* (e.g., *He is gonna do it/He gonna do it*) than in one in which the copula is followed by a noun phrase (e.g., *He is my brother/He my brother*).

External Constraints

External constraints on variation include demographic factors such as region, age, race, gender and socioeconomic level, all factors that have been shown to covary with linguistic factors. Covariance here means that a correlation can be seen between the behavior of a linguistic variable and social factors, so that working-class speakers use more of a variable than middle-class speakers, or African American speakers use a particular variable less than white speakers, and so forth. These correlations make the variation sociolinguistic. Earlier studies of both spoken and sign languages focused on a fairly limited inventory of demographic factors such as those listed above, but, as Wolfram (1997) points out, more recent studies have focused on the nature of communication networks (L. Milroy 1987a), the

117

dynamics of situational context (Biber and Finegan 1993), and the projection of social identity (LePage and Tabouret-Keller 1985) "in an effort to describe more authentically the social reality of dialect in society" (Wolfram 1997, 116). That is, researchers have realized that the external constraints on variation are more complex than they thought. They may certainly include the more discrete factors such as region and socioeconomic level, but other factors such as those with whom a person interacts on a daily basis and a person's desire to project a particular identity to others may also play a central role in constraining variation.

For students of language variation, the examples given above, as well as the many other examples that could be given, raise important questions. Is the variation that we observe in all human languages systematic? If the observed variation is, indeed, systematic, what are the linguistic and social factors that condition a signer's or a speaker's choice among variable linguistic forms? What does the patterning of linguistic and social factors reveal about the underlying grammar of the language under investigation? Are the patterns that we observe stable, or are they the result of ongoing linguistic change? What does linguistic variation reveal about the social structure of the community to which users of the language belong? Finally, what can the study of linguistic variation reveal about the similarities and differences between sign and spoken languages? Is variation in sign languages subject to the same kinds of processes as variation in spoken languages? Are there processes that are unique to sign languages? Are there processes that operate only in spoken languages? Although many outstanding questions remain, particularly with respect to sign languages, after nearly four decades of research on linguistic variation we are in a position to answer the questions posed in this paragraph with considerable confidence, as we show in the following sections.

LINGUISTIC VARIATION IN SPOKEN LANGUAGES

Early Studies of Variation in Spoken Languages

A number of studies of linguistic variation were undertaken before the full development of sociolinguistics as a field in the 1960s. One of the earliest studies was conducted by Gauchat (1905), who correlated changing linguistic features in the French of Charmey, Switzerland, with the age and gender of the speakers. Somewhat later, Fischer (1958) studied the variable use of -*in'* and -*ing* in the speech of New England children. He found that -*ing* was associated with formal situations such as testing and -*in'* with informal interviews. In addition, he found that girls tended to use a greater percentage of the standard form than boys, who typically preferred the -*in'* form. Finally, Fischer noted differences between the speech of "model boys," children who excelled in school and were favored by their teachers, and "typical boys," who were physically strong and domineering. As we might expect, the -*ing* form predominated in the speech of the "model boys," while the -*in'* form predominated in the speech of the "typical boys."

Labov's (1972a) study of language change on the island community of Martha's Vineyard, Massachusetts, marks the transition between early studies of linguistic variation and the development of modern variationist sociolinguistics. Labov studied changes in the pronunciation of the diph-thongs (ay) and (aw)[2] in words such as *spider, pie, fry, mow,* and *outhouse.* These variables were selected because they met the three criteria that Labov had established for a variable to be a useful focus of investigation:

> First, we want an item that is frequent, which occurs so often in the course of undirected natural conversation that its behavior can be charted from unstructured contexts and brief interviews. Secondly, it should be structural: the more the item is integrated into a larger system of functioning units, the greater will be the intrinsic linguistic interest of our study. Third, the distribution of the features should be highly strati-fied: that is, preliminary explorations should suggest an asym-metric distribution over a wide range of age levels or other ordered strata of society. (1972b, 8)

On the basis of interviews with slightly more than 1 percent of the permanent population, stratified by age, ethnicity, occupation and area of residence, Labov found that islanders with the most positive attitudes

Table 1. Centralization and Orientation toward Martha's Vineyard

Persons	Attitude	(ay)	(aw)
40	Positive	63	62
19	Neutral	32	42
6	Negative	9	8

Source: Labov, 1972b: 39.

toward Martha's Vineyard centralized the onsets of these diphthongs most frequently. Speakers with neutral or negative attitudes centralized them much less frequently, preferring instead the pronunciation common among the mainlanders who vacation on the island every summer. The correlation between centralization and attitude toward life on the island can be seen clearly in Table 1. Labov concluded that "when a man says [rəɪt] or [haʊs], he is unconsciously establishing the fact that he belongs to the island, that he is one of the natives to whom the island belongs" (1972b, 36).

Large-Scale Urban Studies

Later in the 1960s, Labov in New York (1966b) and Shuy et al. (1968) and Wolfram (1969) in Detroit carried out studies of sociolinguistic variation on a much larger scale than Labov's original study on Martha's Vineyard. These large-scale urban studies established the systematic nature of a great deal of linguistic variation that had previously been thought to be random, or "free." To illustrate the types of factors that have been shown to influence variation, we will briefly examine three variables: /r/ in New York City, and multiple negation and final consonant cluster reduction in Detroit African American English.

Labov (1966b) studied variation in New York City English in a representative sample of residents of the city's Lower East Side. Among the variables he investigated was the presence or absence of postvocalic (r) in words such as "guard." Although "(r)-lessness" is characteristic of some prestige dialects of English, including upper-class British English, in New York the (r)-less variant is associated with socially stigmatized lower-class speech.

Labov's investigation showed that variation in the pronunciation of postvocalic (r) was strongly correlated with speech style and social class. The data included samples of five speech styles, designed to represent a continuum from a style in which speakers paid the greatest amount of attention to form to a style in which speakers attended only minimally if at all to form: minimal pairs, for example, "god" [gɔːd] and "guard" [gɔɹd], a word list, a reading passage, interview speech and casual speech. The analysis of this extensive corpus of data showed that the more speakers attended to their speech, the more likely they were to pronounce postvocalic (r). Conversely, the more speakers attended to the content of their speech rather than the form, the less likely they were to pronounce (r). Moreover, in each speech style, middle-class speakers were more likely to pronounce (r) than working-class speakers, who in turn were more likely to pronounce (r) than lower-class speakers. That is, the pronunciation of postvocalic (r) showed clear social stratification. Table 2 shows the results for three social classes and five speech styles. These same results are displayed graphically in Figure 1.

These data show that lower-class, working-class and middle-class speakers pronounce postvocalic (r) at different rates. However, speakers of all three social classes may be regarded as members of the same speech community because they are all affected in the same way by an increase in the level of formality and hence in the amount of attention paid to speech. That is, the more careful the style, the more likely they are to use the more prestigious form. Conversely, the less careful the style, the less likely they are to use the prestige form. Thus, New Yorkers, regardless of social class, can be said to subscribe to a common set of linguistic norms, and it is precisely these common linguistic norms that define a speech community in Labov's terms:

The speech community is not defined by any marked agreement in the use of language elements, so much as by participation in

Table 2. (r) Indices for Three Social Classes in Five Styles in New York City

Style	Class		
	Lower class	Working class	Middle class
Minimal pairs	50.5	45.0	30.0
Word list	76.5	65.0	44.5
Reading passage	85.5	79.0	71.0
Interview style	89.5	87.5	75.0
Casual speech	97.5	96.0	87.5

Source: Labov, 1966a, cited in Chambers, 1995.

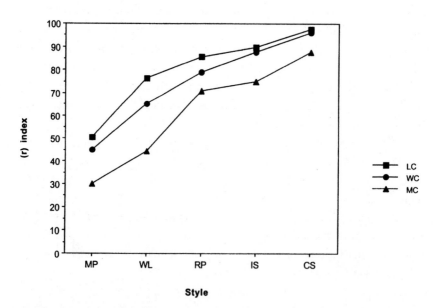

Figure 1. The (r) indices for three social classes in five styles in New York City.
Source: Labov, 1966a, cited in Chambers, 1995.
Notes: (r)-index measures; (r)-less variants. MP—minimal pairs; WL—word list; RP—reading passage; IS—interview style; CS—careful speech. LC—lower class; WC—working class; MC—middle class.

a set of shared norms: these norms may be observed in overt types of evaluative behavior, and by the uniformity of abstract patterns of variation which are invariant in respect to particular levels of usage. (1972b, 120–21)

Numerous studies conducted in cities around the world might serve to illustrate the relationship between use of variable linguistic forms and social structure. These studies range from Harlem in New York City (Labov 1969b, 1972a), Norwich, United Kingdom (Trudgill 1974), and Rio de Janeiro, Brazil (Guy 1981), to Appalachia in the southern USA (Wolfram and Christian 1976) and Compton, California (Baugh 1983). Recent work includes studies of communities ranging from Kingston, Jamaica (Patrick 1999), and San Juan, Puerto Rico (Cameron 1998), to Canterbury, New Zealand (Maclagan et al. 1999), and Xining, China (Dede 1999). Thus, we might have chosen a large number of examples from a wide variety of languages to further illustrate the relationship between use of variable linguistic forms and social structure and the effects of linguistic factors on patterns of variation. However, we shall confine ourselves to two examples, both from African American speakers in Detroit.

Multiple Negation in Detroit

In English, double, or multiple, negation (*He don't want none* vs. *He doesn't want any*) is a well-established and stable sociolinguistic variable. Although every child who has attended school in the English-speaking world is presumably told at some point (or at many points) that use of more than one negative in a clause is ungrammatical and, by false analogy to mathematics, that two negatives make a positive, people persist in saying things like *He don't got none*. Wolfram's (1969) pioneering study of African American English provides a convenient example of the social distribution of this widespread variable. His results, by social class and gender, taken from a large and representative sample, are shown in Table 3.

As in the case of (r) in New York City, use of multiple negation by Detroit African Americans is stratified by social class. Thus, upper-middle-

Table 3. Percentage of Multiple Negation in Detroit African American English by Gender and Social Class

	Upper middle	Lower middle	Upper working	Lower working
Male	10.4	22.3	68.2	81.3
Female	6.0	2.4	41.2	74.3

Source: Wolfram, 1969: 162.

class men use multiple negation only 10.4 percent of the time that they could use multiple negation. In sharp contrast, lower-working-class men use multiple negation more than 80 percent of the time. The situation with women is similar. In Wolfram's data, multiple negation is rare in the speech of middle-class women. Lower-working-class women, however, use multiple negatives 74.3 percent of the time.

Wolfram's study of African American speech in Detroit confirms Labov's (1966b) work in New York with respect to showing that use of variable linguistic forms is correlated with social class. Table 3 also shows a clear gender difference. Not only is use of double and multiple negatives associated with social class, but it is also associated with gender. Although men and some women of all social classes sometimes use multiple negatives, women use fewer multiple negatives than men of the same class.

Like the pattern for social stratification shown for (r)-lessness in New York and multiple negation in Detroit, the gender difference revealed by Wolfram's study has been replicated (see, for example, Trudgill 1974; Milroy and Milroy 1978).

The Case of -t,d Deletion

Final consonant cluster reduction, usually restricted to -*t,d* deletion (the pronunciation of words such as *kind, mist* and *west*, as *kin', mis'* and *wes'*) is among the best-documented variable processes in English. In fact,

Patrick refers to -*t,d* deletion as a "showcase variable" (1999, 122). Among the varieties in which -*t,d* deletion has been studied are AAVE (Labov et al. 1968; Wolfram and Fasold 1974; Baugh 1983), Chicano and Tejano English (Santa Ana 1992; Bayley 1994a, 1997), Jamaican Creole (Patrick 1999), Philadelphia and New York white English (Guy 1980; Labov 1989) and Lumbee English (the dialect spoken by the Lumbee Indians of North Carolina) (Wolfram et al. 2000), to name just a few. Final cluster reduction has been of enduring interest to linguists because it occurs at the intersection of phonological and grammatical processes and thus provides a convenient testing ground for linguistic theories (for a review see Labov 1997, 148–51).

Research has shown that -*t,d* deletion is affected by multiple aspects of the linguistic environment, including syllable stress, the features of the segments that precede and follow -*t,d*, and the grammatical function of the word in which -*t,d* appears. Moreover, although speakers of different dialects delete -*t,d* at very different rates, speakers of most English dialects exhibit remarkable cross-dialectical consistency in the effects of particular factors (for a summary of pan-English constraints, see Labov 1989, 92). For example, as we have seen above, speakers of most English dialects are more likely to delete -*t,d* when it is part of a word stem, for example *the band played on*, than when it is a past-tense morpheme, for example, *they bann/d/ publication of the results*. Speakers are also more likely to delete -*t,d* when it is followed by another consonant, for example *mist by the lake*, than when it is followed by a vowel, for example, *mist in the morning*. That is, -*t,d* deletion is conditioned by both grammatical and phonological factors. An example, from Wolfram's early work in Detroit, is shown in Table 4 and Figure 2.

As Wolfram's data show, not only does the range of -*t,d* deletion in the speech of Detroit African Americans vary as a function of social class, but it is also affected by the linguistic environment. For speakers of all social classes, -*t,d* is most likely to be retained when it functions as a past-tense marker and is followed by a vowel. In this linguistic environment, rates of -*t,d* deletion range from a low of 7 percent among upper-middle-class speakers to a high of 34 percent among lower-working-class speakers.

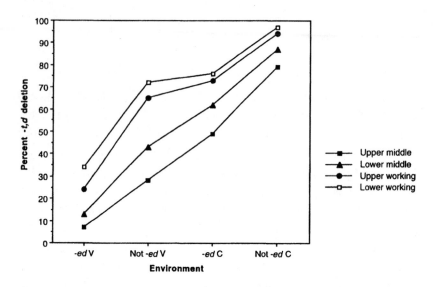

Figure 2. –*t,d* deletion by grammatical class, following environment and social class in Detroit African American English. Source: Wolfram and Fasold, 1974.

Table 4. Percentages of -*t,d* Deletion in Detroit African American English by Linguistic Environment and Social Class

	Social class			
Environments	Upper middle	Lower middle	Upper working	Lower working
Following vowel				
-*t,d* is past morpheme (e.g., "missed in")	7	13	24	34
-*t,d* is not past morpheme (e.g., "mist in")	28	43	65	72
Following consonant				
-*t,d* is past morpheme (e.g., "missed by")	49	62	73	76
-*t,d* is not past morpheme (e.g., "mist by")	79	87	94	97

Source: Wolfram and Fasold 1974: 132.

126

Similarly, for all social classes, -*t,d* is most likely to be deleted when it is not a past-tense marker and when it is followed by another consonant, with rates of deletion ranging from 79 percent among upper-middle-class speakers to 97 percent among lower-working-class speakers.

Recent Research on Sociolinguistic Variation in Spoken Languages

Studies such as those summarized here have served to confirm Weinreich et al.'s (1968) hypothesis that language is characterized by "structured heterogeneity." That is, although all human languages are variable, for the most part variation is not random. Rather, it is systematically constrained by a wide range of social and linguistic factors. Not only has more recent work in language variation expanded the number of language varieties investigated, but researchers have also analyzed social categories in more sophisticated ways and related empirical studies of variation in language communities to developments in contemporary linguistic theory. For example, in most contemporary sociolinguistic studies, gender is no longer viewed as a fixed dichotomous variable. Rather, as in other disciplines, gender is viewed as a social construct that interacts with other aspects of personal identity in particular situations (see, for example, Milroy 1987b; Bucholtz 1999; Eckert and McConnell-Ginet 1999; Eckert 2000). Similarly, ethnicity is no longer viewed as a fixed category. Rather, recent work has explored the ways in which people construct ethnic identities in fluid situations. Rampton (1997), for example, studied the dynamic and shifting perspectives on language and ethnicity of members of multiethnic peer groups in Britain. Schecter and Bayley (1997) examined the diverse ways in which members of Mexican-descent families in California and Texas interpreted, created, and recreated identities as they attempted to reconcile the sometimes conflicting demands of school success for their children and cultural and linguistic continuity. Zentella (1997), in a longitudinal study of the Puerto Rican residents of a single block in East Harlem, New York City, shows in detail how the young women she studied chose among language varieties (e.g., popular

127

Puerto Rican Spanish, standard New York English, AAVE) to express different aspects of their identities, to fulfill expected roles in the community and to accommodate to the linguistic preferences of their interlocutors.

In addition to incorporating more finely nuanced concepts of gender and ethnicity and to drawing upon ethnographic as well as interview data, recent work in sociolinguistic variation has sought to relate the results of empirical studies conducted in the language community to work in formal linguistics. Guy (1991), for example, developed an exponential model, based on lexical phonology (Kiparsky 1982) in order to account for the different rates of retention of final consonant clusters (i.e., $-t,d$) in past-tense, semiweak and monomorphemic clusters. He predicted that final $-t,d$ would be retained in the ratio of x : x2 : x3 as a consequence of a deletion rule operating one, two and three times for words of different morphological classes. The results of empirical study, later replicated by Santa Ana (1992) and Bayley (1997), confirmed the prediction.

More recently, Wilson and Henry (1998) explored the relationship between Chomsky's (1986, 1995) principles and parameters framework and sociolinguistic studies of variation. They suggest that dialects are "constrained and partly defined at the level of grammar by internal operations of the language faculty" (Wilson and Henry 1998, 13) and that understanding parameter settings can enable sociolinguists to understand which structures are likely to change. Finally, the development of optimality theory, which attempts to provide a formal account of variation, has given rise to renewed dialogue between variationist sociolinguists and formal linguists (see, for example, Antilla 1997; Guy 1997; Nagy and Reynolds 1997).

Sociolinguistic Variation and Language Change

Up to this point, we have been concerned with sociolinguistic variation at the synchronic level. However, studies of sociolinguistic variation have also proven important in explaining language change (Labov 1984). It is evident that all living languages undergo change. It is also evident that change does not take place immediately. Rather, new forms are gradually introduced into a language, and, for a considerable period, sometimes lasting for many generations, both old and new forms are in variation. As we would expect, innovative forms are more common in the language of young people than in the language of their elders. This fact has enabled sociolinguists to employ the construct of "apparent time" to model ongoing linguistic change in communities around the world. That is, students of language variation have examined the distribution of older and innovative linguistic forms by age group (as well as other social factors) in order to predict the course of linguistic change.

The work of Bailey and his associates on Texas and Oklahoma dialects of English (Bailey et al. 1991, 1993) offers a convenient example of how studies of synchronic variation may be used to model linguistic change. Bailey and his colleagues drew on random samples of the populations of both states in order to assess the general direction of linguistic change; then they compared their results with data collected fifteen years earlier for the Texas portion of the *Linguistics Atlas of the Gulf States* (LAGS) (Pedersen et al. 1981). The comparison of results for a number of phonological variables validated the apparent time construct. Changes that LAGS indicated were gaining strength, for example, loss of /j/ after alveolars, as in Tuesday ([tju] vs. [tu]), were even stronger among younger speakers in the later studies. Conversely, changes that LAGS had indicated were receding, for example, intrusive /r/ in the word *Washington,* were even rarer in the speech of the youngest participants in the later studies. Comparison of nonphonological variables provided additional confirmation of the utility of the apparent time construct. To take just one example, in the studies conducted by Bailey et al., *fixin' to* had gained strength among younger Texans, as predicted by the LAGS results.

SUMMARY

To summarize, we now know that much of the linguistic variation that was previously thought to be random is highly systematic. That is, although we cannot predict whether any particular instance of a variable form will be realized as one variant or another, we can predict that users of a language who belong to particular social groups generally use more of one variant than users who belong to other social groups and that some variants appear more frequently in certain linguistic environments than in others.

Variation is constrained by both social and linguistic factors. Among the social factors are class, age, gender, ethnicity, educational level, and region of origin. Particularly with respect to factors such as class, gender, and ethnicity, in recent years researchers have sought to incorporate ethnographic perspectives rather than simply to impose preexisting social categories. In this regard, recent research has incorporated many of the original insights of Labov's (1963) pioneering study on Martha's Vineyard, which sought explanations for language change in the local meanings ascribed to linguistic variables. With respect to linguistic factors, research has shown that variation operates at all linguistic levels and that variation may be conditioned by constraints operating at more than one linguistic level, as in the case of -t,d deletion in English. Finally, studies of linguistic variation have contributed greatly to our understanding of language change. The apparent time construct, in particular, has enabled us to model ongoing change by examining the language of people of different ages. Some of the characteristics we observe in teenage language use, particularly in the lexicon, for example, will doubtless be discarded as people move into adulthood. However, some differences between adult and teenage (or younger) language use, especially in phonology, do reflect ongoing changes rather than cohort effects. Since people do not generally alter their basic phonological systems after they have fully acquired their first language, we can predict the course of language change with reasonable confidence.

LINGUISTIC VARIATION IN SIGN LANGUAGES

Since William C. Stokoe's pioneering work in the 1960s, linguists have recognized that natural sign languages are autonomous linguistic systems, structurally independent of the spoken languages with which they may coexist in any given community. This recognition has been followed by extensive research into different aspects of sign language structure and accompanied by the recognition that, as natural sign languages are full-fledged autonomous linguistic systems shared by communities of users, the sociolinguistics of sign languages can be described in ways that parallel the description of spoken languages.

It follows that sign languages must exhibit sociolinguistic variation similar to the variation seen in spoken languages. In the following sections, we review a broadly representative sample of research on variation in ASL and other sign languages.

Variation in ASL

A number of scholars have investigated sociolinguistic variation in ASL, but for the most part their investigations have been limited to small numbers of signers, based on data collected with a wide variety of methods and focused on a disparate collection of linguistic features. Patrick and Metzger (1996), for example, reviewed fifty sociolinguistic studies of sign languages conducted between 1971 and 1994. They found that more than half of the studies involved 10 or fewer signers, and that one third included only one or two signers. Only nine studies involved 50 or more signers, and a number of these drew on the same data set. Patrick and Metzger found that although the number of sociolinguistic studies increased during the period they surveyed, the proportion of quantitative studies declined from approximately half during the period 1972 to 1982 to between one third and one quarter during the period 1983 to 1993. The percentage of studies involving large samples (more then 50 signers) also declined from 33 percent during the first period to just 6 percent during the latter period. The result is that we have yet to have a complete picture of what kinds of units may be variable in ASL and of what kinds of internal and external constraints might be operating on these variable units, although, as Padden and Humphries (1988) observed, deaf people in the USA are aware of variation in ASL, even though it has not been fully described from a linguistic perspective. Padden and Humphries describe:

a particular group of deaf people who share a language—
American Sign Language (ASL)—and a culture. The members
of this group reside in the USA and Canada, have inherited
their sign language, use it as a primary means of communication among themselves, and hold a set of beliefs about themselves and their connection to the larger society. [They continue that] this . . . is not simply a camaraderie with others
who have a similar physical condition, but is, like many other
cultures in the traditional sense of the term, historically created and actively transmitted across generations. (1988, 2)

Certainly there is an ever-growing awareness among its users of the
existence and use of a language that is independent and different from the
majority language, English. ASL users are also aware of sociolinguistic
variation in ASL. However, there are many aspects of that variation that
have yet to be explored. In terms of linguistic structure, many of the studies to date focus on lexical variation, with some studies of phonological
variation, and very few of morphological or syntactic variation. In terms
of social factors, the major focus has been on regional variation, with
some attention paid to ethnicity, age, gender and factors that may play a
particular role in the Deaf community, such as audiological status of parents, age at which ASL was acquired and educational background, for
example, residential schooling as opposed to mainstreaming.

Until very recently, no studies have examined the relationship
between socioeconomic status and variation in a systematic way. So, for
example, there is a widespread perception among ASL users that there are
"grassroots" deaf people (Jacobs 1980) whose educational backgrounds,
employment patterns, and life experiences differ from middle-class deaf
professionals and that both groups use ASL. Accompanying this perception is the belief that there are differences in the variation exhibited in
each group. However, the sociolinguistic reality of these perceptions has
yet to be explored. In this regard, Padden and Humphries state that "even
within the population of deaf people in Boston, Chicago, Los Angeles,
and Edmonton, Alberta [smaller groups] have their own distinct identi-

ties. Within these local communities, there are smaller groups organized by class, profession, ethnicity, or race, each of which has yet another set of distinct characteristics" (1988, 4).

Early Observations and Research on Variation in ASL

Users and observers of ASL have clearly been aware of the existence of variation in the language for a long time, and evidence of this awareness can be seen in writings about deaf people's language use. For example, in 1875, Warring Wilkinson, principal of the California School for the Deaf in Berkeley, wrote about how "the sign language" comes about. He stated:

> The deaf mute child has mental pictures. He wants to convey similar pictures to his friends. Has speech a genesis in any other fact or need? In the natural order of thought the concrete always precedes the abstract, the subject its attribute, the actor the act. So the deaf mute, like the primitive man, deals primarily with things. He points to an object, and seizing upon some characteristic or dominant feature makes a sign for it. When he has occasion to refer to that object in its absence, he will reproduce the gesture, which will be readily understood, because the symbol has been tacitly agreed upon. Another deaf mute, seeing the same thing, is struck by another peculiarity, and makes another and different sign. Thus half a dozen or more symbols may be devised to represent one and the same thing, and then the principle of the "survival of the fittest" comes in, and the best sign becomes established in usage. (1875, 37)

Wilkinson's statement provides some evidence of early awareness of lexical variation, at least among educators of the Deaf, although systematic research did not begin until the 1960s, with Carl Croneberg's two appendices to the 1965 *Dictionary of American Sign Language (DASL)* (Stokoe et al. 1965). "The Linguistic Community" (Appendix C) describes the cultural and social aspects of the Deaf community and discusses the issues of economic status, patterns of social contact and the factors that contribute to group cohesion. These factors include the extensive networks of both a personal and organizational nature that ensure frequent contact even among people who live on opposite sides of the country. Croneberg wrote:

> There are close ties also between deaf individuals or groups of individuals as far apart as California and New York. Deaf people from New York on vacation in California stop and visit deaf friends there or at least make it a practice to visit the club for the deaf in San Francisco or Los Angeles. . . . The deaf as a group have social ties with each other that extend farther across the nation than similar ties of perhaps any other American minority group. (1965, 310)

Croneberg pointed out that these personal ties are reinforced by membership in national organizations such as the National Association of the Deaf (NAD), the National Fraternal Society of the Deaf (NFSD) and the National Congress of Jewish Deaf (NCJD). These personal and organizational patterns of interaction, of course, are central to understanding patterns of language use and variation in ASL.

In "Sign Language Dialects" (Appendix D), Croneberg dealt with sociolinguistic variation, specifically as it pertains to the preparation of a dictionary. As he stated:

> One of the problems that early confronts the lexicographers of a language is dialect, and this problem is particularly acute when the language has never before been written. They must try to determine whether an item in the language is *standard,* that is, used by the majority of a given population, or *dialect,* that is, used by a particular section of the population. (1965, 313)

He outlined the difference between what he termed *horizontal varia-tion* (regional variation) and *vertical variation* (variation that occurs in the language of groups separated by social stratification) and stated that ASL exhibits both. He then described the results of a study of lexical variation undertaken in North Carolina, Virginia, Maine, New Hampshire, and Vermont using a 134-item sign vocabulary list. He found that for ASL, the state boundary between North Carolina and Virginia also constituted a dialect boundary. North Carolina signs were not found in Virginia and vice versa. He found the three New England states to be less internally standardized (i.e., people within each of the three states exhibited a wide range of variants for each item) and the state boundaries in New England to be much less important, with considerable overlap in lexical choice observed among the three states. He pointed out the key role of the resi-dential schools in the dissemination of dialects, stating, "At such a school, the young deaf learn ASL in the particular variety characteristic of the local region. The school is also a source of local innovations, for each school generation comes up with some new signs or modifications of old ones" (1965, 314).

In his discussion of vertical variation, Croneberg mentioned the influence of age, ethnicity, gender, religion, and status. His definition of status encompassed economic level, occupation, relative leadership with-in the Deaf community, and educational background. He further noted that professionally employed individuals who were financially prosperous graduates of Gallaudet University

> tend to seek each other out and form a group. Frequently they use certain signs that are considered superior to the signs used locally for the same thing. Examples of such signs are Gallaudet signs, transmitted by one or more graduates of Gallaudet who are now teaching at a school for the deaf, and who are members of the local elite. The sign may or may not later be incorporated in the sign language of the local or regional community. (1965, 318)

Finally, Croneberg commented on what a standard sign language might be and stated that "few have paid any attention to the term *standard* in the sense of 'statistically most frequent.' The tendency has been to divide sign language into good and bad" (1965, 318), with older signers and educators of the Deaf maintaining the superiority of their respective signs for various reasons. He neatly captured the essence of the difference between prescriptive and descriptive perspectives on language when he wrote, "What signs the deaf population actually uses and what certain individuals consider good signs are thus very often two completely different things" (1965, 319).

As we saw in the quotation that opens this chapter, Stokoe (1994) cited the thinking of George Trager and Henry Lee Smith, who emphasized the connection between a language and its users. The importance of including information about variation in the *DASL* was two-fold. First, the recognition that ASL exhibits variation like other systems that we recognize as languages reinforced the status of ASL as a real language. As a corollary, since variation is often the precursor to change (Milroy 1992), the study of variation in ASL, as in other languages, leads us to an understanding of how the language changes. Second, the inclusion of information about variation in the *DASL*—that is, in a volume that by definition aimed to represent the structure of the language and that was accepted by the community as a reliable representation—reinforces the position that, rather than being just a curiosity or an anomaly, variation is an integral part of the structure of a language. That is, if we are to truly understand the nature of a language, we must account for variation. In this regard, Weinreich et al. (1968), in their work on the role of variation in language change, introduced the idea of orderly or "structured heterogeneity" as the most useful metaphor for understanding the nature of language:

> If a language has to be structured in order to function efficiently, how do people continue to talk while the language changes, that is, while it passes through periods of lessened systematicity? Alternatively, if overriding pressures do force a language to change, and communication is less efficient in the

interim . . . why have such inefficiencies not been observed in practice?

This, it seems to us, is the fundamental question with which a theory of language change must cope. The solution, we will argue, lies in the direction of breaking down the identification of structuredness and homogeneity. The key to a rational conception of language change—indeed, of language itself—is the possibility of describing orderly differentiation in a language serving a community. We will argue that nativelike command of heterogeneous structures is not a matter of multidialectalism or "mere" performance, but is part of unilingual linguistic competence. One of the corollaries of our approach is that in a language serving a complex (i.e., real) community, it is the *absence* of structured heterogeneity that would be dysfunctional. (1968, 99–100)

The inclusion of information about variation in the *DASL*, published in the same era as the early studies of Labov and the pioneering work of Weinreich et al., thus provided a much wider perspective on the fundamental nature of ASL structure and laid the foundation for future investigations.

Lexical Variation

The years following the publication of the *DASL* witnessed a number of studies of lexical variation in ASL. For example, Woodward (1976) examined differences between African American and white signing. His data, based on a small number of signers, included both direct elicitation and spontaneous language production. He suggested that African Americans tended to use the older forms of signs. In 1984, Shroyer and Shroyer published their influential work on lexical variation, which drew on signers across the USA. They collected data on 130 words (the criterion for inclusion of a word being the existence of three signs for the same word) from thirty-eight white signers in twenty-five states. Their findings also included instances of phonological variation, but they did not discuss them as such. They collected a total of twelve hundred sign forms for the 130 words. The 130 words included nouns, verbs, and some adverbs.

Phonological Variation

In the mid-1970s, Battison et al. (1975) examined variation in thumb extension in signs such as FUNNY, BLACK, BORING, and CUTE. All of these signs may be produced with the thumb closed or extended to the side. Thirty-nine signers participated in the study. The social factors determining participant selection were gender, parental audiological status, and the age at which the signer learned to sign (before or after age six). Signers provided intuitive responses as to whether they would extend their thumb in certain signs, in addition to being asked to sign ten sentences under three conditions: "as if" to a deaf friend, "as if" to a hearing teacher, and in a practice situation. In the third condition, signers were asked to practice the sentences and were videotaped doing so without their knowledge. Six internal constraints on thumb extension were reported to distinguish the signs being investigated:

1. indexicality: i.e., is the sign produced contiguous to its referent, as in a pronoun or determiner?
2. bending of fingers: i.e., do the other fingers involved in the sign bend, as in FUNNY?
3. midfinger extension: i.e., is the mid finger extended as part of the sign?
4. twisting movement: i.e., does the hand twist during the production of the sign, as in BORING?
5. whether the sign is produced on the face, as in BLACK or FUNNY
6. whether the sign is made in the center of one of four major areas of the body

All of these features are what Wolfram (personal communication, 1994) would call compositional, that is, features of the signs themselves that may be playing a role in the variation. The analysis found that signs that were *indexic,* such as the second-person pronoun PRO.2 ("you"), had the most thumb extension, followed by signs with bending, such as FUNNY. Signs produced in the center of the signing space, such as PRO.1 ("I"), had less thumb extension. The analysis found no correlation between the linguistic variation and the social factors used to select participants.

Another study of phonological variation, conducted by Woodward et al. (1976), focused on face-to-hand variation, that is, certain signs that are produced on the face in some regions are produced on the hands in other regions. Such signs include MOVIE, RABBIT, LEMON, and COLOR, SILLY, PEACH, and PEANUT. Signers from New Orleans were compared with signers from Atlanta. Data were collected by means of a questionnaire. Results from forty-five respondents suggested that New Orleans signers produced signs on the face that Atlanta signers produced on the hands. Phonological variation can also be seen in the one-handed and two-handed forms of the same sign. Woodward and DeSantis (1977b), for example, examined a subset of such signs produced on the face, including CAT, CHINESE, COW and FAMOUS. They proposed that the features conditioning the variation included outward movement of the sign, high facial location as opposed to low facial location, and complex movement, again all compositional features.

On the basis of questionnaire data, they claimed that the signs that tended to become one handed were those with no outward movement, made in a salient facial area, produced lower on the face, and characterized by complex movement. They also reported that Southerners used two-handed forms more than non-Southerners, that older signers used two-handed signs more than younger signers, and that African American signers tended to use the older two-handed signs more often than white signers of the same age.

Finally, DeSantis (1977) examined variation in signs that can be produced on the hands or at the elbow, such as HELP or PUNISH. The analysis was based on videotapes of free conversation and on responses to a questionnaire. Data for the study were collected in France in the summer of 1975 and in the USA in the spring of 1976. Ninety-nine signers participated, including 60 from France and 39 from Atlanta, Georgia. The results were similar for both French and American signers. Men used the hand versions of the signs more frequently, and women used the elbow versions more frequently.

Morphological and Syntactic Variation

Woodward (1973a, 1973b, 1974) and Woodward and DeSantis (1977a) explored the variable use of three morphosyntactic rules: negative incorporation, agent-beneficiary directionality, and verb reduplication. Negative incorporation is a rule in ASL whereby negation is indicated in a verb by outward movement, as in DON'T-KNOW, DON'T-WANT and DON'T-LIKE, as opposed to KNOW, WANT and LIKE. Agent-beneficiary directionality is the term used by Woodward and DeSantis for verb agreement. For example, in the verb "1st-person-GIVE-to-2nd-person," the hand moves from the signer to a space in front of the signer; in "2nd-person-GIVE-to-1st-person," the hand moves from a space in front of the signer to the signer. What Woodward and DeSantis refer to as verb reduplication entails the repetition of the movement of the verb as a function of aspect, as in STUDY-CONTINUALLY or STUDY-REGULARLY. For the study of these three rules, data were gathered from 141 signers (132 white and 9 African American signers). Other social variables included whether or not the signer was deaf (i.e., some signers were hearing, nonnative signers), whether or not the signer's parents were deaf, the age at which sign language was learned, whether or not the signer had attended college, and gender. Signers were shown examples of the linguistic variables in question and asked to indicate on a questionnaire whether they used the forms presented. The overall results showed that deaf signers who had learned to sign before age six and who had deaf parents used the form of the rules being investigated that was closer to ASL. Internal linguistic constraints were reported only for agent-beneficiary directionality: A continuum of semantic features ranging from "extremely beneficial" to "extremely harmful" was proposed to account for the variation, so that signs like GIVE (beneficial) tend to show directionality, whereas signs like HATE (harmful) do not.

Diachronic Variation

Any review of research on variation in ASL must also include Frishberg's study (1975) of historical development in ASL signs. Frishberg compared signs from earlier stages of ASL and from French Sign Language with present-day usage in ASL to demonstrate that changes have occurred in sign formation. While Frishberg's study is usually viewed as a historical study, it pertains directly to the study of variation in ASL for two related reasons, one general and one specific. The general reason is that historical change manifests itself first in the form of variation. That is, historical change does not occur from one day to the next. Rather, it normally begins as variation, that is, with "different ways of saying the same thing," whether those ways are sounds, parts of signs or grammatical structures, coexisting within the language of an individual or a community.

As mentioned earlier, the focus of variation studies is what Weinreich et al. called "structured heterogeneity," i.e., heterogeneity that is not random but rather governed by internal and external constraints. Moreover, as James Milroy remarked, "In the study of linguistic change, this heterogeneity of language is of crucial importance, as change in progress can be detected in the study of variation" (1992, 1). In some cases, the variation may become stabilized and continue indefinitely, while in other cases, it eventually gives way to the use of one form to the exclusion of the other (or others). Viewed across the broad landscape of history, it may be difficult to see the variation that gives rise to large-scale historical changes, such as the change from Old English to Middle English to Modern English or the changes in Romance languages as they developed from Latin. However, a closer look reveals that change does not happen suddenly and that the transition from one period to the next is characterized by considerable synchronic variation. We may infer that this is the case for sign languages as well. In addition, we suspect that the historical changes that Frishberg described first manifested themselves as synchronic variation.

The second reason for the pertinence of Frishberg's study (1975) to the study of variation is that the processes resulting in historical change that she described are still operative in the language today. She stated:

> Signs which were previously made in contact with the face using two hands now use one, whereas those which have changed from one-handed articulation to two-handed are made without contact on the face or head. Signs which use two hands tend to become symmetrical with respect to the shape and movement of the two hands. . . . As part of a general trend away from more "gross" movement and handshapes toward finer articulation, we find the introduction of new movement distinctions in particular signs, the reduction of compound forms to single sign units, a decreased reliance on the face, eyes, mouth, and body as articulators, and a new context-dependent definition of "neutral" orientation. (1975, xvii)

Frishberg also found:

1. The signs that change from two hands to one are also typically displaced, i.e., change their location from the center of the face and/or from contact with the sense organs, to the periphery of the face;
2. The signs that change from one hand to two hands tend to centralize by moving toward what Frishberg called the *line of bilateral symmetry* (an imaginary line that runs vertically down the center of the signer's head and torso) and up toward the hollow of the neck.

These findings are important because they are described as examples of historical change in ASL. However, some aspects of what Frishberg characterized as historical change, implying perhaps that the change was complete, may be better characterized as change in progress.

RECENT RESEARCH ON VARIATION IN ASL. In recent years, the amount of research on variation in ASL and other sign languages has increased substantially. This body of work includes studies of variation at all linguistic levels, from features of individual segments to discourse units.

Lexical Variation

The work on lexical variation in ASL is quite extensive. In addition to general studies of lexical variation, such as Shroyer and Shroyer discussed in the previous section, the literature contains small-scale studies of various social and occupational categories, most undertaken in the 1990s. Researchers have looked at gender differences (Mansfield 1993), differences in the use of signs for sexual behavior and drug use (Bridges 1993), variation related to socioeconomic status (Shapiro 1993) and lexical variation in the signing produced by interpreters for Deaf-Blind people (Collins and Petronio 1998).

Phonological Variation

Variation in ASL phonology has also received considerable attention in recent years. Metzger (1993), for example, looked at variation in the handshape of second- and third-person pronouns, which can be produced either with the index finger or with an S handshape with the thumb extended. Metzger's data yielded one example of the thumb variant and one unexpected variant, the fingerspelled pronoun S-H-E. There is some indication that the sign that precedes the thumb variant AGO, with its closed handshape, may play a role in the occurrence of the thumb variant.

Lucas (1995) studied variation in location in the sign DEAF. In its citation form (the form of the sign that appears in dictionaries and is most commonly taught to second language learners), the 1 handshape moves from a location just below the ear to a location on the lower cheek near the mouth. However, this sign is commonly produced with movement from the chin location to the ear location or simply with one contact on the lower cheek. Observation might suggest that the final location of the sign (chin or ear) would be governed by the location of the preceding or following sign, so that the sign DEAF in the phrase DEAF FATHER might be signed from chin to ear, since the location of the following sign is the forehead, higher than the ear. Similarly, in the phrase DEAF PRIDE, one might expect that DEAF would be signed from ear to chin, as the sign that follows DEAF begins below the chin.

Contrary to expectations, Lucas's results (based on 486 examples produced by native signers in both formal and informal settings) using the
VARBRUL statistical program[3] indicated that the location of the following and preceding signs did not have a significant effect on the choice of
a variant of DEAF. Rather, the key factor turned out to be the syntactic
function of the sign itself, with adjectives being most commonly signed
from chin to ear or as a simple contact on the cheek, and predicates and
nouns being signed from ear to chin. Pinky (fourth finger) extension
formed the subject of a recent investigation by Hoopes (1998), who studied in detail the signing of one native signer. Some signs that in citation
form have a handshape in which the pinky finger is closed and not
extended variably allow the extension of the pinky. Examples include the
signs THINK, LAZY and CONTINUE. Hoopes's findings, discussed in detail
below, parallel Lucas's finding about the relative lack of importance of the
location of the preceding or following sign. In both cases, the phonological factors that might seem to be most important—location in the case
of DEAF and handshape in the case of pinky extension—in fact did not
appear to condition the variation.

Recently, Kleinfield and Warner (1996) examined ASL signs used to
denote gay, lesbian and bisexual persons. Thirteen hearing interpreters and
twelve deaf ASL users participated in the study. Kleinfield and Warner
focused on eleven lexical items and provided detailed analysis of phonological variation in two signs, LESBIAN and GAY. The analysis showed that
the variation can be correlated to some extent with external constraints
such as the signer's sexual identity (straight or gay/lesbian).

Variation in Fingerspelling

Turning to the area of fingerspelling, Blattberg et al. (1995) examined a
subset of the data from Lucas's project on sociolinguistic variation in ASL
(Lucas et al. 2001). They compared two groups of middle-class signers—
aged 15–25 and 55 and over—from Frederick, Maryland, and Boston,
Massachusetts. They found that both groups of young people used fingerspelling in either full or lexicalized forms and that fingerspelling was

produced in the area below the shoulder generally used for fingerspelling. The young people used fingerspelling primarily for proper nouns and for English terms that have no ASL equivalents. The adults also used finger-spelling for these purposes, but their use of fingerspelling also resembled the use of locative signs. In addition, Maryland adults and adolescents used fingerspelling much more frequently than their counterparts in Massachusetts.

Finally, Mulrooney (2001) found clear evidence of a gender effect in fingerspelling, whereby men were more likely to produce noncitation forms (e.g., produced outside of the usual fingerspelling area) than women.

Discourse

Recently, scholars have begun to investigate variation in ASL discourse. Haas et al. (1995), for example, examined backchanneling, turntaking strategies and question forms in a conversation between Deaf-Blind individuals, comparing them to the same features in sighted ASL signing. They found that "in the tactile mode, Deaf-Blind signers use remarkably similar turn-taking and turn-yielding shift regulators as Deaf-sighted signers" (1995, 130). Touch is often substituted for eye gaze and

> turn-yielding often uses a combination of dominant and non-dominant hands in yielding to the addressee. The dominant hand rests, and the nondominant hand moves to "read" the signer's dominant hand. Turn-claiming occurs with the domi-nant hand of the addressee repeatedly touching or tapping the nondominant hand of the signer until the signer yields and moves their nondominant hand to the "reading" position.

As for question forms, in this particular study, none of the question forms found seemed unique to Tactile ASL. Collins and Petronio (1998), however, found that for yes-no questions, nonmanual signals that in sighted ASL include the raising of the eyebrows are conveyed manually in

Deaf-Blind signing as either an outward movement of the signs or the drawn question mark.

Malloy and Doner (1995) looked at variation in cohesive devices in ASL discourse and explored gender differences in the use of these devices. Specifically, they looked at reiteration and expectancy chains. Reiteration is one type of lexical cohesion that "involves the repetition of a lexical item, at one end of the scale; and a number of things in between—the use of a synonym, near-synonym, or superordinate" (Halliday and Hasan 1976, 278). Expectancy chains have to do with the fact that, in discourse, certain words or phrases are expected to follow certain others. The predictability of their order makes for cohesion. In their analysis of the use of reiteration and expectancy chains in the retelling of a story by two native signers (one male and one female), Malloy and Doner found that the male signer used reiteration more frequently than the female signer but that the signers were similar in their use of expectancy chains.

Research on African American Signing

African American signing has been the object of several recent investigations. Studies include Aramburo (1989), Guggenheim (1992), Lewis et al. (1995) and Lewis (1996). Aramburo and Guggenheim observed lexical variation during the course of structured but informal interviews. Lewis et al. (1995) studied the existence of and attitudes toward African American varieties. Specifically, they described the differences in body movement, mouth movement, and the use of space in the signing of one African American signer who code-switched during the course of a monologue. In addition, they explored how interpreters handled the code-switching in spoken language from Standard English to African American Vernacular English (AAVE). Lewis (1996) continued the examination of African American signing styles in his paper on the parallels between communication styles of hearing and deaf African Americans. His investigation took its departure from two observations: First, ASL users recognize the existence of what is often referred to as "Black signing" but have difficulty in explaining what makes it Black; second, uniquely Black or "ebonic" (Asante 1990) kinesic and nonverbal features exist, and these

146

features occur in the communication of both hearing and deaf African Americans. His investigation described some of these kinesic and nonverbal features—specifically, body postures and rhythmic patterns accompanying the production of signs—in the language used by a deaf adult African American woman. The frequently articulated perspective that African American signing differs markedly from White signing in all areas of structure—and not just lexically—is thus beginning to be explored.

An International Perspective on Variation in Sign Languages

Sutton-Spence and Woll (1999), in their volume on the linguistics of British Sign Language, report on several studies of variation in that language. For example, Woll (1991) found that there were many features that differentiated older and younger signers. Older signers used more fingerspelling and had less clear mouthing patterns than the younger signers. Younger signers showed more influence from English in their signing. These differences are attributed to:

1. the small number of deaf families, making for a discontinuity between generations
2. changes in the educational system for deaf people
3. changing technology

Woll also found lexical differences between older and younger signers and across regions. In terms of family backgrounds, Day (1995) compared British signers from deaf and hearing families and found that their signing differed significantly. Le Master and Dwyer (1991) report on the lexical differences between male signing and female signing found in Dublin, a direct result of segregated schooling for deaf children in Ireland. Sutton-Spence and Woll also describe differences between Roman Catholic and Protestant signers in Britain:

> The signing of British Catholics is strongly influenced by Irish Sign Language (ISL) because Irish monks and nuns have provided education for Catholic deaf children that is suitable for

Catholic beliefs, and Irish-trained priests serve the Catholic Deaf communities in Britain. The Catholic signing uses many initialized signs that are based on the Irish manual alphabet. (1999, 28)

Variation due to religious background extends to the Jewish Deaf in Britain, reported on by Weinberg (1992). There was at one time a school for Jewish deaf children in London that was oral but permitted the use of signing after the arrival of deaf German refugee children in the 1930s. The variety of signing that emerged at this school continued as long as graduates of the school remained in the community and did not associate much with other deaf people. However, it has been little used since the school closed in the early 1960s. More recently, it has been noted that Israeli Sign Language is influencing the signing of British Jewish deaf people, as many Jewish deaf people visit Israel and are increasingly adopting Israeli signs (Sutton-Spence and Woll 1999, 28). In addition, Sutton-Spence and Woll mention that there may be variation correlated with social group identity, i.e., Nigerian, Pakistani or Greek, to name several.

In Italian Sign Language (LIS), Radutzky (1990), while focusing on historical change, described phonological variation. Furthermore, in her 1992 dictionary of LIS, Radutzky makes mention of lexical variation at the regional and inter- and intra-urban levels. Lexical variation is also discussed in Brien and Brennan's work (1995) on the preparation of sign language dictionaries and has been explored by Collins-Ahlgren (1990) in New Zealand Sign Language, by Schermer (1990) in Dutch Sign Language, by Boyes-Braem (1985) in Swiss German Sign Language and Swiss French Sign Language, by Yau and He (1990) in Chinese Sign Language and by Campos (1994) in Brazilian Sign Language.

PERSPECTIVES ON THE STRUCTURE OF SIGN LANGUAGES

Up to now we have concentrated on the results of individual studies. However, the varying perspectives on the basic structure of ASL and of sign languages in general also need to be considered. Current thinking about the linguistic structure of sign languages sheds new light on some of the earlier studies of sign language variation, while at the same time raising important issues for data analysis. For example, the perspective on the fundamental structure of signs has changed dramatically since the earliest studies of variation. Stokoe's perspective, which shaped sign language studies from 1960 until fairly recently, held that signs are composed of three basic parts or parameters (the location at which the sign is produced, the handshape and the movement of the sign) and that, unlike the sequentially produced segments of spoken languages, these parts are produced simultaneously.

In a more recent perspective developed by Liddell (1984) and Liddell and Johnson (1989), signs are viewed as composed of movement and hold segments, sequentially produced, somewhat analogous to the consonants and vowels of spoken languages. We recognize that there is considerable ongoing debate as to the nature of the segments in question (see, for example, Coulter 1992; Perlmutter 1992; and Sandler 1992). However, the Liddell-Johnson framework, as Liddell (1992) amply demonstrates, allows not only for an accurate account of the description of any individual sign but also for an accurate account of phonological processes such as assimilation, metathesis, epenthesis and segment deletion, processes that play central roles in variation.

A central concern of any variation study is to define clearly the linguistic variables being examined and to make sure that they are indeed variable. Current thinking about the linguistic structure of sign languages and about data collection methodology also has implications for the identification of variables in the earlier studies of sign language variation. It is not clear, for example, that the rules of negative incorporation, agent-beneficiary directionality, and verb reduplication in Woodward's (1973a, 1973b, 1974) studies are, in fact, variable in native ASL.

The apparent variability of these rules merits reexamination, as it simply may have been an artifact of combining data from native and non-native signers. For example, in terms of the semantic continuum proposed for agent-beneficiary directionality (from "beneficial" to "harmful"), it may be that directionality is obligatory in most of the verbs in question and is unrelated to semantic considerations. It is basically the way in which agreement is shown with the subject and the object of the verb and is not optional. Failure to use space properly in these verbs would seem to result not in a variable form, but in an ungrammatical one.

While the semantic categorization does seem to work for some verbs (e.g., "beneficial" for GIVE and "harmful" for HATE), it does not work at all for others. For example, it is not clear at all why FINGERSPELL would be labeled as "harmful." It may be that at the time of the study, FINGERSPELL as an agreement verb was an innovation and hence not widely attested, placing it at the "less frequent use of directionality" end of the continuum. But FINGERSPELL cannot therefore be said to have a semantic characteristic of "harmful," the researcher's account of this end of the continuum that he set up.

SIGN LANGUAGES VS. SPOKEN LANGUAGES

Based on the review of research on linguistic variation in sign and spoken language communities, as well as our understanding of the changes in perspective on the nature of sign languages, we are now in a position to compare variation across modalities. In this section, we compare variable units, variable processes and internal constraints in both sign and spoken languages. We then focus on the social constraints that are particular to Deaf communities, as well as on the specific circumstances that need to be taken into account even when evaluating the effect of social constraints that are common to all communities, such as age and gender.

Variable Units in Sign and Spoken Languages

Table 5 compares variability in spoken and sign languages. From this table we can see the same kinds of variability in sign languages as have been described for spoken languages. Specifically, the features of the individual segments of signs can vary. In spoken languages, a consonant may become nasalized or may be devoiced, for example. In sign languages, the

Table 5. Variability in Spoken and Sign Languages

Variable unit	Examples	
	Spoken languages	Sign languages
Features of individual segments	final consonant devoicing, vowel nasalization, vowel raising and lowering	change in location, movement, orientation, handshape in one or more segments of a sign
Individual segments deleted or added	-t,d deletion, -s deletion, epenthetic vowels and consonants	hold deletion, movement epenthesis, hold epenthesis
Syllables (i.e., groups of segments)	aphesis, apocope, syncope	first or second element of a compound deleted
Part of segment, segments or syllables re-arranged	Metathesis	metathesis
Variation in word-sized morphemes or combinations of word-sized morphemes (i.e., syntactic variation)	copula deletion, negative concord, avoir/être alternation, lexical variation	null pronoun variation, lexical variation
Variation in discourse units	text types, lists	repetition, expectancy chains, Deaf-Blind discourse, turntaking, backchanneling, questions

handshape, the location and the palm orientation may vary. Pinky extension or thumb extension in one-handshape signs (PRO.1 ["I"], BLACK, FUNNY) are examples of handshape variation, while signs like KNOW and SUPPOSE provide examples of location variation, as they can be produced at points below the forehead.

Individual segments may be deleted or added. This is seen in spoken English with -t,d deletion. In sign languages, movement segments may be added between holds (as in the phrase MOTHER STUDY) or hold segments may be deleted between movements (as in the phrase GOOD IDEA). Groups of segments (i.e., syllables) can be deleted. The English words *because* and *supposed (to)* are sometimes pronounced as 'cause and 'posed to. The first element of a sign compound, such as the sign WHITE in the compound sign WHITE⌒FALL ("snow"), is often deleted, and many signers are not even aware of its existence. Parts of segments, segments or syllables can be rearranged. As mentioned earlier, English speakers sometimes pronounce the word hundred as "hunderd." In sign languages, this can be seen in the location feature of the sign DEAF. That is, the sign may begin at the ear and end at the chin or vice versa. Everything else about the sign is the same, but the location feature is rearranged. And there can also be variation in word-sized morphemes, otherwise known as lexical variation, and in combinations of word-sized morphemes, i.e., syntactic variation. Variation has also been described in bigger units, that is, in the units of discourse. In spoken languages, for example, researchers have described variation in the way speakers use lists in discourse (Schiffrin 1994) and variation in sign language discourse has also been explored (see discussion above of Haas et al. 1995; Malloy and Doner 1995). The one kind of variation that we have not seen in sign languages yet is coalescence, whereby a new segment is created from the features of other segments. We see this in English, for example, when the sound *sh* (/ʃ/) is created by the interaction between *t* and *i* in the word *demonstration*. The *sh* sound is created and the original segments disappear.

In addition, while we assume that syntactic variation exists, there is very little research in this area. Although Woodward (described earlier) claimed that there was variation in three syntactic rules, the data upon which the claim is based combine the signing of native and nonnative signers. However, one kind of syntactic variation in sign language involves variable subjects with plain verbs. That is, in addition to the many verbs in sign languages in which the pronominal information is incorporated into the structure of the verb (e.g., GIVE or FLATTER in ASL), there are many so-called plain verbs (Padden 1988) (e.g., LIKE or KNOW in ASL) that would seem to require the production of separate signs for subject and object. However, ASL is a "pro-drop" language. That is, the subject and object pronouns that accompany plain verbs are variably deleted (Lucas et al. 2001).

Finally, in terms of what kinds of units can be variable, we have noticed one kind of variability that seems to be an artifact of a language produced with two identical articulators, i.e., two hands as opposed to one tongue. That is, sign languages allow the deletion, addition or substitution of one of the two articulators. Two-handed signs become one handed (ASL CAT, COW), one-handed signs become two handed (ASL DIE), and a table, chair arm or the signer's thigh may be substituted for the base hand in a two-handed sign with identical handshapes (ASL RIGHT, SCHOOL). Variation is also allowed in the relationship between articulators, as in the ASL sign HELP, produced with an A handshape placed in the upward-turned palm of the base hand. Both hands can move forward as a unit, or the base hand can lightly tap the bottom of the A handshape hand.

Variable Processes in Spoken and Sign Languages

In Table 6, variable processes are summarized for both spoken and sign languages. Here, we see that the same kinds of processes that pertain to spoken language variation also pertain to sign language variation: processes of assimilation, weakening, substitution and addition, and analogy. We see assimilation, for example, when a 1 handshape in the sign PRO.1 ("I") becomes an open 8 handshape in the phrase PRO.1 PREFER ("I prefer").We also see it in the compound sign THINK⌢MARRY ("believe"), in which the palm orientation of the sign THINK assimilates to the palm orientation of

Table 6. Variable Processes in Spoken and Sign Languages

Process	Examples	
	Spoken languages	Sign languages
Concerning the phonological component of languages		
Assimilation	Vowel harmony, consonant harmony, germination, nasalization	Assimilation in handshape, location, orientation
Weakening	Deletion, CC reduction, haplology, aphesis, syncope, apocope, vowel reduction	Hold deletion, deletion of one articulator, first or second element of a compound deleted
Substitution, Addition	3rd person singular –s	Add second hand to one-handed sign
Concerning morphosyntactic structures		
Co-occurrence relations	Negative concord	Possibly nonmanual signals
Item permutation	Adverb placement	Possibly placement of interrogative words

154

the sign MARRY. We see weakening when holds are deleted or when a two-handed sign becomes one handed, as in CAT or COW. Substitution can be seen when a table top or the signer's knee is substituted for the base hand of a two-handed sign or in the version of the sign DEAF that begins at the chin and moves to the ear, as opposed to beginning at the ear and moving to the chin. Addition is seen when movements are added between holds. Finally, the process of analogy is seen when a one-handed sign becomes two handed.

In terms of morphosyntactic variation, we may expect to find variation in co-occurrence relations, as found in spoken languages. Recall the example of the co-occurrence of negative items in spoken English, so that a sentence such as "Ain't nobody seen nothing like that before," with three negative items co-occurring, is acceptable in AAVE, while the sentence "No one has seen anything like that before," with only one negative element, is preferable in middle-class standard English. We are not exactly sure what variable co-occurrence relations might look like in ASL, but a possible candidate for investigation is the co-occurrence of nonmanual signals with lexical signs or with morphological or syntactic units. For example, must a given nonmanual signal (such as the mouth configuration in the sign NOT-YET) co-occur with the manual sign? Is there any variation in the morphological and syntactic nonmanual signals that occur with manual adverbs and sentences? Another kind of morphosyntactic variation concerns the fact that certain items—for example, adverb placement in spoken English—can occur in different positions in a sentence. Again, item permutation is an area that has yet to be explored in sign languages. One possible candidate in ASL is the placement of interrogative signs (WHO, WHERE, WHAT, WHEN, WHY, FOR-FOR) in sentences and also their repetition.

Internal Constraints on Spoken and Sign Languages

Table 7 summarizes the internal constraints on variable units. Earlier studies of variation in ASL focused on compositional constraints. That is, variation was seen to be conditioned by some feature of the variable sign

Table 7. Internal Constraints on Variable Units in Spoken and Sign Languages

Constraint	Examples	
	Spoken languages	Sign languages
Compositional	Phonetic features in nasal absence in child language	Other parts of sign in question e.g., handshape, location, orientation
Sequential	Following consonant, vowel, or feature thereof	Preceding or following sign or feature thereof
Functional	Morphological status of –s in Spanish –s deletion	Function of sign as noun, predicate, or adjective
Structural incorporation	Preceding or following syntactic environment for copula deletion	?syntactic environment for pronoun variation
Pragmatic	Emphasis	Emphasis (e.g., pinky extension)

itself. For example, Battison et al. (1975) hypothesized that thumb extension in signs such as FUNNY or BLACK was conditioned by the number of other fingers extended, the secondary movement of the sign and other features of the sign itself. Sequential constraints are those that have to do with the immediate linguistic environment surrounding the variable, such as the handshape or palm orientation of the sign immediately preceding or following the variable sign, as we see with 1 handshape signs. Functional constraints have to do with the role that the function of the sign has in the variation, as we will see in our discussion of the ASL sign DEAF. The constraint of structural incorporation has to do with the preceding or following syntactic environment surrounding the variable. One would consider structural incorporation as a constraint when trying to understand what conditions the variable subjects in plain verbs, for example PRO.1 LIKE vs. (PRO.1) LIKE. Finally, pragmatic features may act as constraints. As we will see below, Hoopes (1998), for example, found that the lengthening of a sign for emphasis played a role in the occurrence of pinky extension. Emphasis is a pragmatic factor, a feature chosen by the signer in a particular context to convey a particular meaning. It is not an inherent feature of the sign.

Furthermore, a fundamental difference between sign language variation and spoken language variation may be emerging from the analysis of internal constraints. This difference relates to the fact that variation in spoken languages is for the most part a sequential phenomenon; that is, it is a phenomenon that affects linguistic segments which occur in sequence, segments occurring at the boundaries of larger units, i.e., words. The examples of -t,d deletion and the (-ing) variable discussed above are representative of this phenomenon.

It is beginning to be clear that sign languages make considerably less use of affixation, such that deletable final segments may not be morphemes in the same way that they are in spoken languages. The past-tense marking accomplished by the -t or -d in English or the plural marking accomplished by -s is accomplished in different ways in ASL. Similarly, verb agreement is not accomplished by affixation as in many spoken languages, but rather by a change in the location and/or palm orientation feature of one segment of a sign. There are many agreement verbs in ASL, and there are also plain verbs, i.e., verbs that do not allow agreement to be incorporated into the location or orientation feature of the verb and that require separate lexical signs for subject and object.

There is some anecdotal evidence for plain and agreement variants of the same verb, for example, CALL-ON-TELEPHONE. But since verb agreement is not accomplished by the sequential affixation of morphemes, the internal constraints on such variation will have nothing to do with the sequential occurrence of morphemes, as it does in Caribbean Spanish, for example, with final -s aspiration and deletion in verbs. Clearly, we will most likely have to search elsewhere in the linguistic environment for some of the internal constraints on variation.

Social Constraints Particular to Deaf Communities

Social constraints like gender, age and ethnicity have been examined in numerous studies of sociolinguistic variation. However, many of these constraints need to be articulated more fully when they are put into research practice in a particular community. This is especially true for studies of linguistic variation in Deaf communities. Notions like socio-economic status or even age cannot simply be borrowed whole from studies of variation in spoken language communities. The differences in social constraints when applied to Deaf communities are of two types: First, there are constraints like age whose labels have a common application, but which might have a different meaning considering the history of Deaf communities around the world; second, there are constraints, like language background, that are unique to Deaf communities.

Considering constraints of the first type, definitions of gender, age, regional background and ethnicity need to be reevaluated in studies of Deaf communities. For deaf people, regional background, or where they grew up, may be less significant than where their language models acquired a natural sign language or where they attended school, i.e., if this was a residential school, or if it was oral or used a sign language as a medium of instruction. Age as a sociolinguistic variable may have different effects on linguistic variation because of the differences in language policies in Deaf schools in the twentieth century. Thus, while differences in the signing of older and younger people may appear to be due either to age group differences or to natural language change (such as occurs in all languages), these differences may also be the result of changes in educational policies, like the shift from oralism to "total communication" (i.e., manualism) that occurred in the USA, or from total communication to a bilingual-bicultural approach. These language policies affected not only what language was used in the classroom, but also teacher hiring practices (deaf signers of ASL, or hearing teachers who knew no ASL). These language policies affected deaf children's access to appropriate language models, and this access may have varied across time to such an extent as to affect the kind of variation we see in sign languages today.

With respect to ethnicity, demographics and oppression may work doubly against our understanding of language use in minority deaf communities. The linguistic and social diversity in the Deaf community is just beginning to be explored by researchers (Lucas 1996; Parasnis 1998), and many questions remain about how ethnic minority deaf people self-identify and how they use language. Are the boundaries of these groups such that they form coherent groups whose ethnic identity is stronger than their Deaf identity? Or do the members of these groups construct a separate minority Deaf identity? Is it reasonable to acknowledge multiple potential language influences? Is the use of a particular variant related to a person's identity as a deaf person or as an African American deaf person, for example? Through the social network technique of contacting potential informants, Lucas et al. (2001), described in more detail below, uncovered one way in which ethnicity and age have intersected to create a situation of oppression multiplied. Lucas et al. were unable to find any African American deaf people over age 55 who were members of the middle class, that is, who had a college education and were working in professional occupations. This finding suggests that political, social and economic factors intersect with race and ethnicity in ways that have profound effects on minority language communities like the Deaf community.

With respect to gender, several questions emerge that are also related to the minority language community status of Deaf people. Those yet to be answered include the following: Is there a solidarity in language use between men and women in a language minority group because of oppression from the outside and shared experiences rooted in being deaf? Or are usage differences as pronounced as in other communities?

Other differences in social constraints arise from the unique characteristics of Deaf communities. The question of the language background of signers who participate in studies is one such characteristic. Most participants in variation studies acquired the language under study as a native language from native-speaking parents, as well as from exposure in their everyday environment. In Deaf communities, some participants had neither of these kinds of exposure to the language at the earliest stages of their development. Even deaf parents may not be native signers. It may seem that this problem conflicts with the goal of describing the use of a particular language. However, if all signers who learned a natural sign language from people other than their parents were excluded from sociolinguistic studies, such studies would be invalidated because they would not be representative of the community. Researchers should simply take account of the language background of their participants while drawing conclusions from the data. If the analysis is qualitative, the language background of the participants should be expressly stated in the report and accounted for in the analysis. If the analysis is quantitative, the influence of language background differences on the variables being investigated may be included as a factor in the statistical model.

A related constraint is the school background of informants. Whether the signers attended a residential or mainstream school may influence their signing. Some questions related to this issue are the following: Did the signers acquire a natural sign language at a very early age from signing adults, or did they learn it at a later age, having entered the community later? At what age did they acquire the sign language in use in their community? Did their language models use an artificial system such as Signed Exact English (SEE) or the natural sign language of the community?

THREE RECENT STUDIES OF VARIATION IN ASL

A number of recent studies of linguistic variation in sign languages reflect the changing perspective on the nature of sign languages. In this section, we describe three of these studies: Hoopes's study of pinky extension, Collins and Petronio's (1998) study of variation in Tactile ASL, the language of the U.S. Deaf-Blind community, and Lucas et al.'s study (2001) of variation in the form of the sign DEAF. The three studies all adopted theoretical frameworks that incorporate recent insights into the nature of ASL. They also illustrate the range of contemporary investigations into variation in ASL and other sign languages. Hoopes (1998) is an exploratory case study based on data from a single signer. Collins and Petronio's (1998) study is also exploratory. The authors aimed to understand the parameters of variation in the language variety of a group that had not previously been studied systematically. Lucas et al. (2001) is a large-scale study based on a representative sample of the U.S. Deaf population.

An Exploratory Case Study of a Phonological Variable

Signing with one's pinky extended on some signs has been anecdotally discussed as a possible phonological variable. Signs like THINK, WONDER, and TOLERATE (the latter two illustrated in Figures 3a and 3b) can be signed either with the pinky (the fourth finger) closed or fully extended. Hoopes (1998) sought to determine whether pinky extension showed patterned variation that correlated with phonological, syntactic or discourse constraints and to consider functional explanations for these correlations. He set out to describe this potential variable as part of one individual's signing style and to discuss possible constraints on the use of pinky extension (PE). In this study, Hoopes decided to focus on the signing of a single individual because, as numerous studies have shown, individuals normally use all of the variants that are common to their community, even within the same conversation (Guy 1980).

The signer for this study was a fifty-five-year-old Euro-American deaf woman who was deafened in infancy; she was the only deaf member of

(a) Wonder, +cf   Wonder, –cf

(b) Tolerate, +cf   Tolerate, –cf

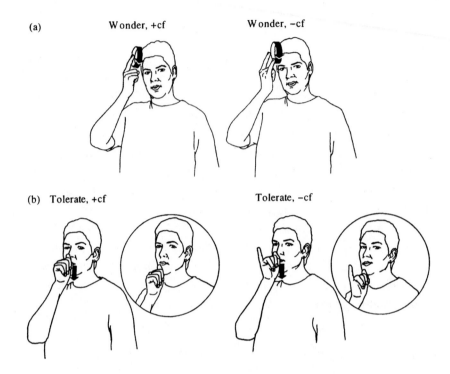

Figure 3a, b. WONDER, TOLERATE, citation and noncitation forms

her immediate family. She attended a residential school and Gallaudet
University. She was videotaped in conversation in four separate sessions,
each lasting one to two hours, creating a total of seven hours of conversational data. Her conversational partners included a close friend and deaf
and hearing interlocutors.

For the analysis, Hoopes extracted one hundred occurrences of pinky
extension from the videotaped data. Each of these occurrences was coded
for the following linguistic and social factor groups:

1. preceding handshape
2. following handshape

3. sign in which PE occurs
4. discourse topic
5. handshape of the PE sign
6. syntactic category of the PE sign
7. level of intimacy between informant and conversational partner

A subset of these occurrences was also coded for prosodic features. This coding involved timing the duration of the tokens by the number of frames each lasted. These durations were averaged and then compared with the duration of tokens of the same lexemes (i.e., signs) without pinky extension. The following possible constraints were investigated for this subset of tokens:

1. duration of the sign
2. preceding or following pause
3. repetition of the sign

Some potential occurrences were excluded from the pool of tokens. Occurrences in fingerspelling were excluded because it was assumed that in these cases PE resulted from processes other than those that could cause pinky extension in lexical signs. Also excluded were instances of "lexicalized" pinky extension, in which case the non-PE variant and the PE variant would not co-occur in the signing of one individual. Lastly, signs in which pinky extension did not occur over the full production of the sign were excluded.

The analysis of the full 100 tokens, not including the prosodic analysis, consisted of comparing percentages of tokens in each of the subgroupings of the constraints. In the prosodic analysis, Hoopes compared the average duration of the signs with and without pinky extension.

The findings indicated that the frequency of occurrence of pinky extension did in fact vary and did correlate with linguistic factors (handshape and syntactic category) and the one social factor analyzed (degree of social distance). The most intriguing finding, however, was that pinky extension tended to co-occur with prosodic features of emphatic stress.

Specifically, it tended to occur:

1. with lexemes used repeatedly within a discourse topic
2. before pauses
3. with lexemes lengthened to almost twice their usual duration

This suggests that pinky extension is itself a prosodic feature of ASL that adds emphatic stress or focus to the sign with which it co-occurs. It is quite analogous to stress in spoken language as indicated by a stronger signal as a result of greater articulatory effort.

It should be noted that sociolinguistic methodology was crucial to this last finding, i.e., that pinky extension played a prosodic function in the variety used by the subject. Prosody has largely been ignored by linguists working within either the Chomskian or the earlier structuralist framework due to the tendency of these frameworks toward categoricity. Prosody tends not to be subject to categorical rules. But, as Hoopes's study shows, when one searches for factors that constrain, but do not absolutely determine, the occurrence of a linguistic form, the patterning of prosodic features emerges.

Exploring the Dimensions of Variation: A Study of Tactile ASL

A second recent study looked at the signing of Deaf-Blind people, known as Tactile ASL. While the ASL of sighted deaf people has been studied for forty years, the signing of Deaf-Blind people is a new subject of linguistic research. Collins and Petronio (1998) set out to describe changes in signing that occur when ASL is used in a tactile, rather than a visual, mode. The goal was to describe the particular variety of ASL used in the Deaf-Blind community, when Deaf-Blind people converse with other Deaf-Blind people. The authors considered that variation between sighted ASL and Tactile ASL could occur at any level of linguistic structure.

To collect representative samples of Deaf-Blind conversation, Collins and Petronio used two sets of conversational data, one relatively informal and one relatively formal. Informal data were collected at a party attended by eleven Deaf-Blind people. The more formal data came from another set of conversations between three pairs of Deaf-Blind people, all using Tactile ASL to tell stories to each other. The seventeen signers had all been born deaf, known and used ASL prior to becoming legally blind, become blind as a result of Usher's Syndrome I, and regularly socialized with Deaf-Blind adults who use Tactile ASL. Tactile ASL can be received with one or both hands. In order to limit the possible variation that could occur even within Tactile ASL, only one-handed conversations were included in the data set.

Collins and Petronio focused on the differences and similarities of the phonological form of signs used in visual and Tactile ASL. (Space does not permit a discussion of the findings pertaining to morphology, syntax and discourse, but a full account can be found in Collins and Petronio 1998.) Signs were examined in terms of their handshape, location, movement and orientation. Early studies on visual ASL sought minimal pairs to determine the distinctive parts of signs. Minimal pairs were interpreted as providing evidence for three parameters: handshape, location and movement. For instance:

- handshape: The signs DONKEY and HORSE use the same location and movement but differ in handshape.
- location: MOTHER and FATHER use the same handshape and movement but differ in location.
- movement: SICK and TO-BECOME-SICK use the same handshape and location but differ in movement.

Battison (1978) later identified a fourth parameter, orientation, based on pairs such as CHILDREN and THINGS. These two signs have identical handshape, location and movement. However, they differ in the palm orientation: The palm of the hand faces upward for THINGS but toward the floor for CHILDREN. Using these four parameters, Collins and Petronio examined signs in the Tactile ASL data to see if there were any phonological differences between the same sign when it was used in visual ASL.

Collins and Petronio found no variation or changes in the handshape parameter. The other three parameters (movement, orientation and location) displayed the same type of variation due to phonological assimilation that occurs in visual ASL. However, although the same forms of variation occurred in Tactile ASL, this variation was sometimes due to the receiver's hand being on the signer's hand and the physical proximity of the signer and the receiver. For example, because of the physical closeness, the signing space used in Tactile ASL was generally smaller than that used in visual ASL. This smaller space usually results in smaller movement paths in signs. In addition, because the signer's and receiver's hands were in contact, the signing space shifted to the area where the hands were in contact; correspondingly, the location of signs articulated in neutral space also shifted to this area. The orientation parameter showed some variation that resulted from modifications the signer made to better accommodate the receiver. One change, unique to Tactile ASL, occurred with signs that included body contact. In addition to the signer's hand moving toward the body part, the body part often moved toward the hand in Tactile ASL. This adaptation allowed the receiver to maintain more comfortable tactile contact with the signer.

The variation, adaptations and changes that Collins and Petronio described are examples of linguistic change that has occurred and is continuing in the U.S. Deaf-Blind community. In the past several years, in addition to an expansion of the American Association of the Deaf-Blind, there has been growth in chapters of this organization based in various states. Deaf-Blind people are increasing their contact with other Deaf-Blind people. The opportunity for Deaf-Blind people to get together and form communities has resulted in sociolinguistic changes in ASL as Deaf-Blind people modify it to meet their needs. From a linguistic viewpoint, Tactile ASL provides us with a unique opportunity to witness the linguistic changes ASL is experiencing as the Deaf-Blind community adapts the language to a tactile mode.

A Large-Scale Quantitative Study: Lucas et al. (2001) on DEAF

We began this chapter with observations about variation in the ASL sign DEAF. These observations are based on the results of a large-scale study of variation in ASL (Lucas et al. 2001) that analyzed phonological, syntactic and lexical variation. Conversational ASL was videotaped in seven sites around the USA (Massachusetts, Virginia, Maryland, Louisiana, Kansas/Missouri, California and Washington state). Participants were from three age groups (15–25, 26–54, 55+) and included male and female, Caucasian and African American, and working-class and middle-class signers. The analysis of the sign DEAF is based on 1,618 examples taken from the data. Although the sign DEAF has many possible forms, only three of these forms were extracted from the videotapes. In citation form (+cf), the sign begins just below the ear and ends near the corner of the mouth. A second variant begins at the corner of the mouth and moves upward to the ear. This variant was labeled the "chin to ear" variant. In the third variant, the "contact cheek" variant, the index finger contacts the lower cheek but does not move up. The three variants are illustrated in Figures 4a, 4b and 4c.

These variants were compared using a multivariate statistical program that requires many examples as input but which allows the researcher to investigate the effects of many potential constraints at the same time. Results of the analysis of the 1,618 examples indicated that variation in the form of DEAF is systematic and conditioned by multiple linguistic and social factors, including grammatical function, the location of the following segment, discourse genre, age and region. The results confirmed the earlier finding of Lucas (1995), which showed that the grammatical function of DEAF, rather than the features of the preceding or following sign, is the main linguistic constraint on variation.

The analysis was divided into two stages. In the first stage, the citation form was compared with the two noncitation forms. In the second stage, the two noncitation forms were compared with one another. For the choice between citation and noncitation forms, among the linguistic factors, only grammatical function and discourse genre proved to be

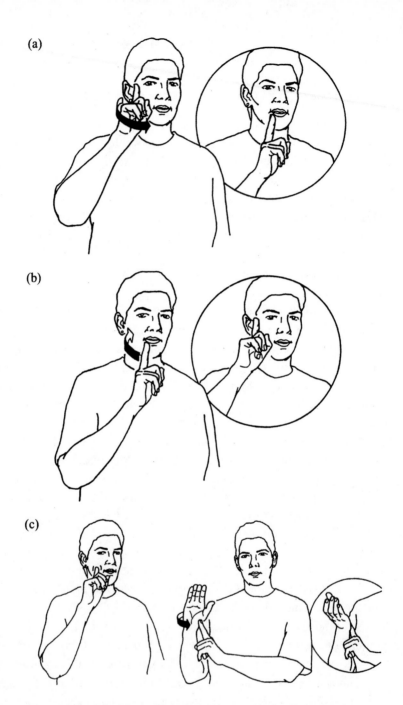

Figure 4a, b, c. DEAF, ear-to-chin, chin-to-ear, contact-check (DEAF CULTURE)

statistically significant. For the choice between the two noncitation forms, both the grammatical function of DEAF and the location of the following segment proved significant. Among the social factors, only age and region contributed significantly to the observed variation. The other nonlinguistic factors for which the researchers coded—ethnicity, gender, language background and social class—failed to reach statistical significance.

Specifically, while the youngest and oldest signers in four of the seven sites (Virginia, Louisiana, California, and Washington) preferred noncitation forms, in these sites signers aged 26 to 54 were more likely to use citation forms. In one site (Kansas/Missouri) the noncitation form was favored by signers in all age groups, while in another (Massachusetts) noncitation forms were disfavored by signers in all age groups. Finally, in one site (Maryland) older signers preferred the noncitation forms, while the middle-aged and younger ones preferred the citation form. The results clearly show that DEAF is a classic sociolinguistic variable, and the challenge for researchers is to explain the correlation between the linguistic factors and the social ones. One explanation directly concerns the history of Deaf education in the USA.

The history of Deaf education has had a direct impact on the recognition of ASL as a language, independent in structure from English. Before 1880, while opponents questioned its status, ASL was widely accepted as the medium of instruction. Between 1880 and 1960, however, the status of ASL was very fragile, even among its users. Recall that in 1960 William Stokoe published the first linguistic description of ASL (Stokoe 1960), and the recognition of ASL as a viable natural language slowly began to grow. The history of Deaf education and the recognition of ASL appear to be reflected in the patterns of variation in this study. Specifically, in the majority of sites studied, older signers use more noncitation forms. Many of them were attending residential schools at a time when ASL was actively suppressed and forbidden. While they were certainly fluent users of the language, there was very little metalinguistic awareness or prescriptivism accompanying that use. Indeed, many of the older signers in the study could not provide a name for their language—ASL—as the two younger groups could. Rather, many of the older signers still referred to their fluent language production simply as "sign."

In contrast, the 26- to 54-year-old signers in the sample were in school at the time when ASL was beginning to be recognized and valued as a language separate from English. ASL was still not accepted in classrooms, but there was a rapidly growing awareness in the Deaf community of the need for recognition. In the late 1960s and early 1970s, formal instruction in sign language began, along with the preparation of teaching materials. This new awareness of the status of ASL helps explain the preference among the 26- to 54-year-old signers in the majority of sites examined for the citation forms of DEAF.

The prescriptivism seen here in the use of citation forms may be regarded as a tool in maintaining the hard-won recognition of ASL. Finally, the youngest signers in the sample all attended school at a time when, for the most part, the status of ASL was no longer in question. The change in the status of ASL may explain the more frequent use of noncitation forms by younger signers. The status of the language is not threatened by the use of noncitation forms. This would seem to account for the general patterns that we see. Deviations from this pattern, such as the preference in the older Massachusetts signers and the youngest Maryland signers for citation forms, may be explained by the specific history of those communities, which is now being explored.

Other policy changes in Deaf education may also play a role in the patterns exhibited in the data. For example, in recent years, educational policies in many U.S. states have favored placing deaf children in mainstream public school classes (Ramsey 1997). As a result of such policies, children have fewer opportunities to interact on a daily basis with communities of ASL users. In addition, the Deaf community in the USA has long been characterized by its own social institutions and by dense social networks (Baynton 1996).

SUMMARY OF THE STUDIES

The three studies reviewed here are examples of current work being carried out on variation in sign languages. This is work that reflects changing perspectives on sign language structure and use. The studies of DEAF and of pinky extension, in particular, show us that the analysis of internal constraints on variation in ASL needs to proceed with caution, as the identification of such constraints may not always be completely straight-forward. While casual observation might suggest the presence of phono-logical constraints, further examination reveals functional constraints (as in the case of DEAF) or pragmatic ones (as in the case of pinky extension). The analysis of DEAF highlights the importance of considering the social factors particular to Deaf communities.

Methodological Issues for the Studies

The three recent studies discussed also illustrate the methodological issues that need to be considered when studying linguistic variation. Three of the main issues are:

1. defining and sampling a community
2. describing natural language
3. defining variables and constraints

We will discuss each one in turn, with particular attention to the implications for the study of sign languages.

Defining and Sampling a Community

The first issue common to studies of variation in both sign and spoken languages concerns sampling. The goal of all variation studies is to describe the patterns of variable linguistic structure within and across language communities. Whether the study is qualitative or quantitative, participants in the study must be members of the communities whose language use is being described. Further, quantitative sociolinguistic work that seeks to reach conclusions about language use in a community as a whole must take steps to ensure that its participant group is as representative as possible of the entire community.

A study of variable sign language use in the Deaf community, for example, must study the language use of deaf people who use the particular sign language being studied. The language community may be defined in both linguistic and social terms. If the study finds that a group of ASL users have some aspect of their language in common—for example, if the constraints on a particular variable affect all members of the community in the same way—then this is evidence that that group is a linguistic community (Labov 1972b). When defining the language community in social terms, variation studies have taken two main approaches. One approach is to use broad social categories, like socioeconomic status and gender, to draw boundaries around subgroups within a community (Labov 1966b, 1972b). Another is to use community-based social networks. This latter approach looks at a community in terms of the number and nature of connections among individuals in order to correlate these connections with patterns of language use (Labov 1972a; Milroy 1987a, 1987b; Eckert 1989). A researcher who employs either approach, however, has an explicit definition of the language community in terms of common social factors.

The three recent studies described above examine variation in language structure and use in the U.S. Deaf community. The researchers in each case took steps to ensure that all participants were deaf users of ASL and that they were all connected socially to their local Deaf communities. In Hoopes's (1998) study of pinky extension and Collins and Petronio's (1998) study of Tactile ASL, the participants were known by the researchers to be members of local Deaf communities. They had grown up as users of ASL, attended residential schools and participated in social relationships with other deaf people and in Deaf organizations like Deaf clubs. In Collins and Petronio's study, it was also important that participants be members of a community of Deaf-Blind people. The researchers defined this membership both in terms of physical blindness and in terms of language use and socialization. All seventeen participants were legally blind as a result of Usher's Syndrome I, all regularly socialized with other Deaf-Blind adult users of Tactile ASL, and all were comfortable and experienced users of Tactile ASL.

In Lucas et al.'s (2001) study not all participants in the seven communities were personally known to the researchers. Rather, the project relied on contact people in each area to recruit a sample that was as representative of the community as possible. This strategy was informed by the social network approach of Milroy (1987b). Potential participants were approached by a contact person; this was a deaf individual who lived in the area, who possessed a good knowledge of the local community and who was a respected member of the community. A major concern of this study was representativeness. Therefore, the researchers and contact people tried to recruit a group of participants diverse enough to match the diversity of the U.S. Deaf community.

Describing Natural Language

The second issue concerns the type of data analyzed. Studies of sociolinguistic variation differ in a fundamental way from formal studies of abstract linguistic competence; studies of variation are committed to studying language in context (Labov 1966b, 1972b; Milroy 1987a, 1987b; Lucas 1995). Directly eliciting different variants of a sociolinguistic variable would defeat the purpose of studying how the social and linguistic environments of language use condition variation. The sociolinguistic interview, although it has been used in many studies as a way in which linguists could record conversational language use, has been criticized as not being conducive to "natural speech" (Milroy 1987b; Schilling-Estes 1999). The ideal would be to record and study the full range of the community's styles of language use, from formal lectures given to an audience of strangers, to casual daily encounters with friends and acquaintances. In reality, this is impossible. First of all, few people, if any, whether they are deaf or hearing, sit around waiting for linguists to come and record their conversations. Also, as we discuss further below, the camcorder would be distracting.

Despite these fundamental limitations on linguists' access to "natural language use," each of the three recent studies reported on here made methodological accommodations toward gathering conversations that were as natural as possible. The conversation types that were recorded differed on many dimensions: how well the conversational participants knew one another, the degree to which the conversations were about language itself, the length of the conversations, and the presence or absence of the researchers during the videotaping. Each of these dimensions might have provided an environment that would affect variation. For this reason, the conclusions take into account these aspects of the recorded conversations.

Hoopes, for example, recorded the signer during four different one-to two-hour conversations with other ASL users. The first and third conversations were with a close friend of hers, also deaf, from her residential school. The second recording was made during a conversation with a deaf graduate student from Gallaudet University, someone with whom the signer was casually acquainted. During these conversations, the deaf signer and her conversational partner were asked to "just chat." The final conversation was with a hearing interpreter, a good friend of the signer. Before this conversation, the researcher suggested some topics they might discuss. During all of these conversations, the researcher was not a participant; in fact, he was absent from the room.

In their study of Tactile ASL, Collins and Petronio relied on conversational data videotaped under two different circumstances. The first recording was made during an informal party, which lasted about four hours. Eleven Deaf-Blind adults who regularly socialized together attended the party. The researchers videotaped their Tactile ASL conversations with one another. The second situation was one that one of the researchers had set up for an earlier study. In this situation, three pairs of Deaf-Blind adults were recorded telling stories to one another using Tactile ASL. The researcher viewed this second set of data as coming from more formally situated language use.

In Lucas et al.'s study, groups of signers were videotaped during one-to-two-hour data collection sessions. These sessions were divided into three parts. The first consisted of approximately one hour of free conversation among groups of participants, without the researchers present. In the second part, at least two participants were selected from each group and interviewed in depth by deaf researchers about their educational and linguistic backgrounds, social networks and patterns of language use. The final part involved eliciting lexical variants from the participants who had been interviewed. All participants in this part of the data collection were shown the same set of thirty-three pictures and asked to supply signs for the objects or actions represented in the pictures.

Defining Variables and Constraints

The third issue that the studies described here share with all studies of sociolinguistic variation is a concern that what is being investigated is, in fact, a sociolinguistic variable. The three studies are on a frontier, as they are some of the first studies of variation in ASL in about twenty years. The hope is that we now know enough about the structure of ASL in order to (1) to identify what varies, (2) to describe this variation and (3) to quantify it. The first steps in variation analysis are to define the variable and the envelope of variation. That is, what forms count as instances of the variable? Are the forms that vary indeed two ways of saying the same thing?

The three studies required, first, a consideration of what features were noticeably variable. These variables might be found at any level of linguistic structure, from phonology to discourse. For a quantitative study like that by Lucas et al., the hope was that these variables would also correlate with both linguistic and social factors. For qualitative studies like that by Collins and Petronio, in which a language variety is being described in detail for the first time, the goal is that the variables that are described will uniquely identify the community being studied and will be amenable to further quantitative or applied work.

An additional issue that arises early in a variation study concerns specifying the factors that may potentially influence a signer's choice of a variant. Lucas (1995), for example, investigated the potential effects of eight separate linguistic factors on the choice of a variant of DEAF. As it turned out, most of these constraints proved not to be statistically significant. However, the labor of coding for many factors was not in vain. The study demonstrated that Liddell and Johnson's (1989) hypothesis that variation in the form of DEAF is influenced primarily by the location of the preceding sign is, at best, incomplete.

The studies discussed in detail here are at different stages in the process of identifying constraints. Collins and Petronio's study, because its purpose was simply to describe the differences between visual and Tactile ASL, set out to note features that were known to be unique to tactile signing. The researchers knew that being Deaf-Blind is a conditioning factor for some changes in language use, but the question was "what linguistic changes take place?" Hoopes and Lucas et al., on the other hand, needed to propose constraints, both linguistic and social, on the variables to be quantified. A central theoretical issue for variation studies is the identification of internal constraints on the variables. As Labov states, the issue "is to discover whatever constraints may exist on the form, direction or structural character of linguistic change" (1994, 115). Phonological constraints on the variables considered by Hoopes and Lucas et al. could include the segmental phonological environment or suprasegmental, or prosodic, environment. Other linguistic constraints could be morphological, syntactic or related to discourse topic or type of discourse.

As for social constraints, the researcher's knowledge of the community should inform what factors are considered in the model of variation. Hoopes did not design his study of pinky extension to take into account social constraints other than the level of intimacy between conversational partners, as it was expressly limited to investigating the variable signing of a single individual. Collins and Petronio's study suggests that if Deaf-Blind and sighted individuals are included in the same study of variation in ASL, then this should be taken into account, as the sighted or blind status of a deaf person could affect how they use the language. Owing to the much larger sample size, Lucas et al. were able to include several social factors in the statistical analysis of variants of DEAF.

Finally, data collection itself presents a methodological problem. While one goal of sociolinguistic research is to base conclusions on conversation that is as "natural" as possible, one aspect of the basic method required for doing careful study of natural language use impinges on this goal. That is, the conversation being studied needs to be recorded, and yet the fact that the conversation is being recorded makes it less likely to be close to the vernacular use of the language. Labov (1972b) has called this problem the "Observer's Paradox." When one considers sociolinguistic research in Deaf communities, this problem may be magnified.

Videotaping is more intrusive than audiotaping. Equally important is the issue of anonymity. While voices on an audiotape cannot easily be connected to a face or a name, except by the researchers, faces on a videotape are not anonymous. The Deaf community is small, and signers may be concerned, with good reason, that what they say on videotape will be seen by others in the community and understood out of context. With videotaping, complete anonymity is impossible.

CONCLUSIONS

We return now to the questions that we posed at the beginning of this section. It would seem that the variation that we observe in all human languages, whether spoken or signed, is for the most part systematic. The linguistic factors that condition the variation have to do with features of the variable in question, the immediate linguistic environment in which it occurs, its function, or with features of the discourse in which it occurs. While many of the social factors that condition variation are the same for spoken and sign languages—e.g., region, age, gender, ethnicity, socioeconomic class—it seems that there are some factors, such as language use in the home, that are unique to sign language variation. Furthermore, it is clear that age and region need to be understood specifically within the context of Deaf education. While we see many similarities between the variable units and processes in spoken and sign languages, fundamental differences between the respective structures of spoken and sign languages are reflected in variation. We see this in the strong role that grammatical constraints play in phonological variation in sign languages. Continuing research on variation in a wide variety of sign languages can only enhance our understanding of variation in all languages.

SUGGESTED READINGS

For spoken language variation, Wolfram's (1991) *Dialects and American English,* Trudgill's (1999) *Dialects of England,* and Wolfram and Schilling-Estes's *American English* (1998) all provide comprehensive and accessible discussions of the nature of variation, along with clear examples. A more philosophical discussion can be found in Milroy's (1992) *Linguistic Variation and Change*. For sign language variation, Lucas (1995) and Sutton-Spence and Woll (1999) provide good reviews of the literature, and individual articles on variation appear in various volumes of the *Sociolinguistics in Deaf Communities* series (ed. Ceil Lucas; published annually by Gallaudet University Press).

EXERCISES

1. What is variation? What is a sociolinguistic variable?
2. What is a linguistic variable?
3. Explain the concepts of internal constraints and external constraints on variation.
4. Does sign language variation resemble spoken language variation? If so, how?
5. Pick two signs, one which shows handshape variation and one which shows variation in palm orientation. Over the course of several weeks, keep a note of how signers are producing these two signs and of the characteristics of the signers, i.e., male or female, old or young, African American or white, etc. Describe the patterns that emerge from your observations and discuss any external constraints (e.g., ethnic origin, religious affiliation) unique to your situation that may be contributing to the variation you observe.
6. Pick two signs which show regional variation, such as BIRTHDAY or PICNIC. Ask twenty signers what their signs are and make a note of where the signers are from. Again, describe any patterns that emerge from your observations.
7. Do a videotaped interview with two people (at the same time), asking them about topics of interest to the Deaf community, topics that are likely to elicit the sign DEAF. Describe any patterns that emerge, in terms of the sign being produced from ear to chin, from chin to ear, or as a contact on the cheek. If the sign DEAF does not display such variation in the sign language you are analyzing, substitute another sign that interests you.

NOTES

1. In accord with convention, English glosses of ASL signs are written in small capitals.

2. In the notation that has become conventional in sociolinguistics, linguistic variables such as (ay) and (aw) are enclosed by parentheses. Thus, (r), for example, means "variable r." Chambers explains that "the parentheses are intended as equivalents to slashes for phoneme(s) . . . and square brackets for phone(s). . . . Like the phonemes /r/ and /æ/, the variables (r) and (eh) represent abstract linguistic entities. Just as phonemes are actualized as one or more allophones, so variables are actualized as one or another of the variants" (1995, 17).

3. VARBRUL is a specialized application of the statistical procedure known as logistic regression. The program allows the researcher to investigate simultaneously the influence of the many factors that may potentially influence a language user's choice among variable linguistic forms. VARBRUL was developed by David Sankoff (Cedergren and Sankoff 1974; Rousseau and Sankoff 1978). For information on the mathematical basis of the program see Sankoff (1988). For a guide to the use of the program in studies of linguistic variation, see Young and Bayley (1996).

Index

Page references in **boldface** indicate figures/tables/charts

AAVE. *See* African American
Vernacular English
Abbé de l'Epée, 10
AFRICA sign, **47, 51,** 52–53
African American signing, 6, 35, 86,
87, 88–92, 146–47, 159; "Black"
signing, 88, 146; versus Caucasian
signing (lexical variation), 51–52,
83–110, **97, 99, 100, 101,**
137–38; code-switching, 87, 146
African American (spoken English):
multiple negation study, 123–24,
124; -*t,d* deletion study, 124–27,
126
African American Vernacular English
(AAVE), 66, 87, 117, 125, 146, 155
age: as social constraint, 158–59
agent-beneficiary directionality, 140,
141, 149–50
ALWAYS sign, **15**
American Association of the Deaf-
Blind, 166
American Asylum for the Deaf and
Dumb. *See* American School for
the Deaf (ASD)
American Manual Alphabet, **98**
American School for the Deaf (ASD),
10, 11, **50,** 51, 77

American Sign Language (ASL):
compounding, 6-7; five basic parts
of, 12; historical development in
ASL signs study, 141–42;
interpreters, 79, 146; introduction
of new symbols, 6; pro-drop
language, 19, 153; pronoun use in,
44–45, **45;** use of symbols in, 4–6,
4; verbs and, 41–42
arbitrary form (of symbols), 5
ARREST sign, **47, 51,** 52
assimilation (phonological processes),
149
Australian Sign Language (AUSLAN),
6

BANANA sign, 19, 46, **47, 48, 49, 51,**
52
BELIEVE sign, 32
Bell, Alexander Graham, 78
bilateral symmetry, line of, 142
BIRTHDAY sign, 17, 19
BLACK sign, 138, 152
"Black" signing, 88, 146
BOOK sign, 6
BORED sign, 17
BORING sign, 138
Boston signers, 112

Braidwood Schools, 10
Brazilian Sign Language, 148
British Catholic signers, 147–48
British Jewish Deaf, 148
British Protestant signers, 147–48
British Sign Language (BSL), 6, 147

CAKE sign, **47, 51**, 52
California School for the Deaf
    (Berkeley), **50**
California School for the Deaf,
    (Riverside), **50**
CANDY sign, **47, 51**
CAT sign, **4**, 139, 155
categorical difference, 20
Caucasian signing: versus African
    American signing (lexical variation),
    51–52, 83–110, **97, 99, 100, 101,**
    137–38
CEREAL sign, **47, 51**
CHAIR sign, 12, **13**
CHEAT sign, **47, 51**
CHERRIES sign, **47, 51**
Chicano English, 125
CHICKEN sign, **47, 51**
CHILDREN sign, 165
Chinese dialects, 75
CHINESE sign, 139
Chinese Sign Language, 148
citation form, (+cf), 27, 29, 69, 71,
    111, 170; chin to ear, 167, **168;**
    contact cheek, 167, **168;** ear to
    chin, 167, **168;** examples of, **160**
classifier predicates, 6
Clerc, Laurent, 10, 51, 77
coalescence, 152

code-switching, 87, 146
Cogswell, Alice, 10
COLOR sign, **15,** 139
communication: recording
    communication styles, 173–74,
    176–77; styles of, 8–9
communication system, 3, 4, 5
COMPLAIN sign, 12
compositional constraints, 117, **156.**
    See also internal constraints
compositional features: in
    phonological variation, 138–39
compounding, 6
COMPUTER sign, **47, 51**
CONGRESS sign, **15**
Connecticut Asylum for the
    Education and Instruction of Deaf
    and Dumb Persons. *See* American
    School for the Deaf
constructed action (syntactic variation),
    43
constructed dialogue (syntactic
    variation), 43
CONTINUE sign, 144
contrastive, 12
Convention of American Instructors
    of the Deaf, (Fourth), 64
co-occurrence, 155
covariance, 117
COW sign, 139, 155
Croneberg, Carl, 63, 64, 65–66, 68,
    79, 84, 85–86, 133–36
CUTE sign, 12, **13,** 138

Deaf-Blind signers, 21, 58, 143, 145,
    146, 164–66; social constraints

particular to, 158–61; study of
variation in Tactile ASL, 161,
164–66, 172, 174, 176
Deaf education: history of, 77–78,
169–70
DEAF FATHER sign, 143
Deaf President Now campaign, 76
DEAF PRIDE sign, 143
DEAF sign, 14, 15, 16, 20, 25, 27, 28,
29–30, 31, 33, 69, 70, 71, 72, 75,
111, 143–44, 152, 167–70;
distinction between capital "D"
and lowercase "d", 110; linguistic
influence, 31; study of variation,
161, 167–70, 168; 170–76
Deaf Way conference (1989), 67
DEER sign, 18, 32, 47, 51, 52
deletion of -t, d. See -t,d deletion
DELICIOUS sign, 47, 51
demographic factors, 117
descriptive perspective, 20, 136
Detmold, George, 76
Detroit African American English,
120; multiple negation study of,
123–24, 124; -t,d deletion study
of, 124–27, 126
diachronic variation, 141–43
dialect: sociolinguistic variation and,
134–35
dictionary form. See citation form
Dictionary of American Sign Language,
The (DASL) (Stokoe, Casterline,
and Croneberg), 63, 64, 66, 67,
68, 76, 78, 84
Dillingham, Abigail, 11
DIZZY sign, 32

DOG sign, 18, 47, 51
dominant hand, 4, 5
DONKEY sign, 165
DON'T-LIKE sign, 140
DON'T-KNOW sign, 140
DON'T-WANT sign, 140
DRY sign, 12, 13
Dutch Sign Language, 148

EARLY sign, 47, 49, 51
education: history of Deaf, 169–70
educational constraint, 160
Education of All Handicapped Children
Act of 1975. See Public Law 94-142
English glosses. See glosses
English influence (syntactic variation),
43, 44, 45
epenthesis (phonological processes),
18, 149
ethnicity, 127, 159
expectancy chain, 146
external constraints, 113, 117–18. See
also social constraints

face-to-hand variation, 139
FAINT sign, 47, 51
FAMOUS sign, 139
FATHER sign, 32, 165
FATHER STUDY sign, 18
FEAR sign, 47, 51, 52
FEDERAL sign, 32
FEEL sign, 12
FINALLY sign, 14
FINGERSPELL sign, 150
fingerspelling: definition of, 110;
study in variation, 144–45

5 handshape, 20, 35–37, **36**
Flat O handshape, 4, 5
following sign, 33–34, 37
FOR sign, 32, **32**
French Sign Language, 10, 11, 77, 86, 141
functional constraints, 117, **156**, 157. *See also* internal constraints
FUNNY sign, 17, 138, 139, 152

Gallaudet signs, 66, 85, 135
Gallaudet, Edward Miner, 78
Gallaudet, Thomas Hopkins, 10, 51, 77
Garretson, Mervin, 76
GAY sign, 144
gender, 127, 160
gender differences, 145, 146
geographic influences, 112
glosses, 43, 110, 179
GLOVES sign, **47, 51, 52**
GOOD IDEA sign, 18, 152
GOOD sign, 18
grammatical constraints, 71, 74
grammatical function, 33, 37, 70–71, 72

HALLOWEEN sign, 17, 19
handedness, 86
handshape, 86; as basic part of ASL, 12, 14; location of, 143; seven basic forms of the passive hand, 5; Stokoe system, 149; variation in Tactile ASL, 165-66. *See also* 5 handshape, L handshape, 1 handshape
HAPPY sign, 12
HELP sign, 18, 139

holds: as basic part of ASL, 14, 18; definition of, 14. *See also* segments
Hong Kong Cantonese, 75
horizontal variation, 65, 85, 135
HORSE sign, 165

iconic forms, 5
IDEA sign, 18
indexical function, 71
indicating verbs, 41
influential factors, 120–27
(ing) variable, 157
internal constraints, 113, 116–17, 138, 155–58, 170–71; compositional constraints, 117, 156; definition of, 116–17; functional constraints, 117, 156, 157; linguistic constraints, 140; pragmatic constraints, 156, 157; sequential constraints, 117, 156, 157; structural incorporation, 117, 156, 157
international variations, 147–48
interpreters, 79, 146
Irish Sign Language, 147
Israeli Sign Language, 148
Italian Sign Language, 148
ITALY sign, 7, 7

Jamaican Creole, 125
JAPAN sign, **47, 51,** 52–53
Japanese Sign Language, 53, 104

KNOW sign, 17, 18, 20, 25, 32, **32, 34, 35,** 69, 70, 73, 75, 140; linguistic influence, 34; social influence, 35

L handshape, 20, 35–37, **36**
Labov, William, 66, 119–20, 176;
New York City English study of
sociolinguistic variation and the
postvocalic (r), 120–21, **122**, 124;
Observer's Paradox, 54, 176–77
language background: as social
constraint, 158
language: characteristics of, 6–9;
regional differences in, 8; rule-
governed communication system,
3–6; social influences of, 8;
unrestricted number of domains
in, 7; use of symbols in, 4–6
LATE sign, 12
LAZY sign, 144
LEMON sign, 139
LESBIAN sign, 144
lexical signs, 71
lexical variation, 19, 83–110, 132,
135, 137–38, 143, 152; African
American signers compared to
Caucasian signers, 51–52, 83–110,
97, 99, 100, 101, 137–38;
phonologically related variants in,
46, **48,** 49; separate variants in, 46,
47, 49
L handshape, 20, 35–37, **36**
LIKE sign, 140
line of bilateral symmetry, 142
Linguistic Atlas of the Gulf States
(LAGS), 129
"Linguistic Community, The"
(Croneberg) 84, 133–34
linguistic constraints, **72,** 75
linguistic variables, 17, 179;

distinguished from sociolinguistic
variables, 113
linguistic variation: research methods,
171–77
*Linguistics and Language Behavior
Abstracts,* 79
loan sign, 7
location signs: 30, **32,** 33–34, 37
location, 12, 14, 17–18, 86, 165–66
Lumbee English, 125

Manually Coded English (MCE), 11
MARRY sign, 155
Martha's Vineyard, (Massachusetts),
10–11, 66, 119–20
Massieu, Jean, 10
metathesis (phonological processes),
18, 149
MICROWAVE sign, **47, 51,** 52
Milan, Italy, 77
Milroy, Lesley, 113, 173; on
sociolinguistic variables, 13
minority deaf communities, 159–60
MISS sign, 14
MITTENS sign, **47, 51**
modality differences, 22
MONEY sign, 4–5
morphological/syntactic variation, 132,
140–41
morphology, 74
morphosyntactic rules, 140, 155
Morse code, 4, **4**
MOTHER sign, 165
MOTHER STUDY sign, 152
movement, as basic part of ASL, 12,
14, 18; definition of, 14, 18;
variation in Tactile ASL, 165-66

movement epenthesis, 18
MOVIE sign, 139
multiple negation: Detroit African American English and, 123–24, 124

National Association of the Deaf (NAD), 65, 134
National Congress of Jewish Deaf (NCJD), 65, 134
National Fraternity Society of the Deaf (NFSD), 134
natural language: description of, in linguistic variation research, 173–75; Observer's Paradox and, 176–77
negative incorporation, 140, 149
New York City: linguistic variation in spoken languages, 66, 120–22, 125
New Zealand Sign Language, 148
noncitation form, 27, 29–30, 11, 145, 169; examples of, **162**
nondominant hand, 4, 5
nonindexical lexical signs, 71
nonmanual signals, 155; as basic part of ASL, 12, 14
NOT YET sign, 12, 14
number of hands (variation), 18

Observer's Paradox, 54, 176–77
Ohio School for the Deaf, 11
one-handed signs, 139, 152, 153
1 handshape, 25, 35–39, **36**, 69, 70, 71, *72*, 75, 153; linguistic influences, **38**; social influences, **39**
Open B handshape, 5

Open 8 handshape, 153
optimality theory, 128
oral method, 90
oralism, 77, 78, 90; definition of, 110
orientation: variation in Tactile ASL, 165-66
Oxford English Dictionary, 67

PAH sign, 12, 14, **14**
palm orientation, 12, 14, 18, 153, 165–66
PANTS sign, (men's), **47, 51**
PANTS sign, (women's), **47, 51**
parameter of signs, 86
passive hand: seven basic handshapes, 5
PEACH sign, 139
PEANUT sign, 139
Peet, Harvey, 64
Pennsylvania Institution, 11
PERFUME sign, **47, 51**
person and number (syntactic variation), 42
Philadelphia White English, 125
phonological processes, 149
phonological variation, 17, 68, 72, 75, 132, 138–40, 143
pinky extension, 144; Hoopes's study of, 161, **162**–64, 170–71, 172
PIZZA sign, 46, 47, 49, **51**
plain verbs, 42
postvocalic (r): variation in New York City English, 120–21, **122**, 124
pragmatic constraints, 156, 157. *See also* internal constraints
preceding sign, 33–34, 37

prepositions, 6
prescriptive orientation, 20, 136
PRO.1 PREFER sign, 153
PRO.1 sign, 19, 112, 152, 153
PRO.1 THINK sign, 19
PRO.2 sign, 19
pro-drop language, 19, 153
pronouns (linguistic & social
    influences), 45
prosody, 164
Public Law 94-142, 90
PUNISH sign, 139

RABBIT sign, 47, 51, 52, 139
RED sign, 12, 13
regional variation, 132, 169, 170. See
    also horizontal variation
registers, 8
Registry of Interpreters for the Deaf,
    79
reiteration chain, 146
RELAY sign, 47, 51
REMEMBER sign, 32
RIGHT sign, 18
ROOSTER sign, 49
Royal Institution for the Deaf (Paris),
    10
rule-governed system, 3–4
RUN sign, 47, 51

same-reference situation (syntactic
    variation), 42, 44
sampling: in linguistic variation
    research, 171–73
SANDWICH sign, 47, 51, 52
SCHOOL sign, 15

second-person pronouns, 143
segment deletion, 149
segments, 74–75; as basic part of
    ASL, 14, 18; definition of, 14
semantic continuum, 149–50
sentence structure variation, 41–45
sentence type (syntactic variation), 43
sequential restraints, 117, 156, 157.
    See also internal constraints
shift regulators, 145
SHORT sign, 12, 13
SICK sign, 12, 165
sign compound, 152
"Sign Language Dialects" (Croneberg)
    84–85, 134–35
sign languages: horizontal variation,
    65, 85, 135; internal constraints
    on, 155–58, 156; social
    constraints, 158–61; suppression
    of, 77; variable processes in,
    153–55, 154; variable units in,
    150–53, 151; versus spoken
    languages, 150–61; 151, 154, 156;
    vertical variation, 65, 85, 135
sign structure, 15
sign vocabulary list (134-item), 85,
    87, 135
Signing Exact English (SEE), 11
signs: basic parts of, 18–19, 149;
    distinctive parts of, 165; Liddell-
    Johnson framework, 149; location
    of, 143–44; parameter of, 86;
    rearrangement of sign parts, 18
SILLY sign, 139
SIT sign, 12, 13
Smith, Henry Lee, 67, 136

SNOW sign, 18, 49, 47, **51,** 52

social constraints, 57, 113, particular to Deaf communities, 158–60. *See also* external constraints

social factor variation, 30, 37

sociolinguistic variable, 113

sociolinguistic variation: history of variation research, 66–67; international perspectives, 147–48

Sociolinguistic Variation Project, 1–2; demographics of, 25, **26,** 55, 89–91, **93, 106;** contact persons, 91; findings, 92–103, 105; goal of project, 26, 56, 106–7; overview of data collection, **26;** research sites of, 23, **24,** 25, **26,** 50, 88–89, **106;** videotaping, 25

SOON sign, 47, **51**

spoken languages, 5, 74, 75; early studies in variation, 118–27; external constraints on variation in, 117–18; internal constraints on variation in, 116–17, 155–58, **156;** Martha's Vineyard study, 119–20, **120;** multiple negation in Detroit study, 123–24, **124;** postvocalic (r) pronunciation in New York City, 120–21, **122,** 124; recent studies in variation, 127–28; sociolinguistic variation and language change, 128–29; -*t,d* deletion in Detroit, 124–27, **126;** urban studies on sociolinguistic variation in, 120–27, **122, 124, 126;** use of symbols in, 4–6; variable processes in, 115–16, 153–55, **154;** variable

units in, 113–15, 150–53, **151; 154, 156**

SQUIRREL sign, **47, 51**

Standard English, 146

STEAL sign, **47, 51,** 52

stimuli (34 signs), 49, **51**

Stokoe, William, 11, 67–68, 76, 79, 111, 136, 149, 169

Stokoe system, 149

structural incorporation, 117, **156,** 157. *See also* internal constraints

structured heterogeneity, 68, 127, 136–37, 141

STUDY sign, 18

styles (of human communication), 8–9

SUMMER sign, 12, **13**

Swiss French Language, 148

Swiss German Sign Language, 148

switch-reference situation (syntactic variation), 42, 44

syllable deletion, 18

symbols: arbitrary forms of, 5; iconic forms of, 5; language and, 6–8; used in language, 4–6, **4**

synchronic variation, 129, 141

syntactic variation, 19, 43, 114, 132, 152–53; definition of, 41

-*t,d* deletion, 69, 152, 157; Detroit African American English and, 124–27, **126**

TABLE sign, 5

Tactile ASL, 58, 145; study on, 61, 164–66, 172, 174, 175–76

Tejano English, 125
THIEF sign, **47**, **51**, 52
THINGS sign, 165
THINK sign, **15**, 19, 144, 153, 162
thirty-four stimuli, 46, 47, 49, **51**
thumb configurations, 138–39
thumb extension, 138–39
TO-BECOME-SICK sign, 165
TOLERATE sign, 161, **162**
TOMATO sign, **47**, **50**, 52
Total Communication, 25, 90, 110, 159
Trager, George, 67, 136
TRAIN sign, 12, **13**
transcription, conventions of, 43
TREE sign, 5
turn-taking, 145
turn-yielding, 145
two-handed signs, 5, 139, 153

UGLY sign, 12
UNDERSTAND sign, 14
urban studies: sociolinguistic variation in spoken languages, 120–27, **122**, **124**, **126**
Usher's Syndrome I, 165, 172

VARBRUL, 71, 72, 144, 179
variable linguistic forms: gender and,

124; influential factors, 120–27; social class and, 121–22, 124
variable processes: in sign and spoken languages, 153–55, **154**
variable units: in sign and spoken languages, 150–53, **151**
variation, definition of, 18
verb agreement, 140
verb reduplication, 140, 149
vertical variation, 65, 85, 135
videotaping (research participants), natural language use and, 173–74; Observer's Paradox and, 176–77
vocabulary list (134 signs), 85, 87, 135

WANT sign, 140
WEEK sign, 18
WHITE sign, 18, 49, 52
WHY sign, 32
WONDER sign, 17, **162**, 172
Woodward, James, 66, 67, 79
WORD sign, 4–5
word-sized morphemes. *See* lexical variation
word-sized units (variation of), 19, 114. *See also* lexical variation
WRONG sign, 5

YESTERDAY sign, 17, 20